SAMSON'S STORY

A ~~Tail~~ Tale of Pet Loss Grief, Love, Hope and Magic

GALE WILKINSON

Copyright © 2025 by Gale Loves Dogs, Inc.
All rights reserved.

No portion of this book may be reproduced in any form without written permission from the author or publisher.

This book is sold with the understanding that neither the author nor the publisher is engaged in rendering psychological, legal, financial, medical, or any other professional services or advice. While the author and publisher have used their best efforts in preparing this book, they make no representations or warranties with respect to the accuracy or completeness of the contents of this book and specifically disclaim any implied warranties of merchantability or fitness for a particular purpose. The advice and strategies contained herein may not be suitable for your situation. Readers are responsible for obtaining such advice from their own professional counsel when appropriate. Neither the author nor publisher shall be liable for any loss of profit or any other commercial damages, including but not limited to special, incidental, consequential, personal, or other damages.

Book cover art and design by Jessica Badofsky.
Typesetting and page design by Jessica Badofsky.
Copy editing by Timothy Johnson.

Hardcover ISBN: 979-8-9985881-0-5
Paperback ISBN: 979-8-9985881-1-2
epub ISBN: 979-8-9985881-3-6

Library of Congress Control Number: 2025906988

First edition. 2025.

www.petlossgrief.info

I dedicate this book to Samson, to your dear pet, and to all the other loving pets who have and will leave us much sooner than we'd like.

Introduction	9
1. Saying Goodbye	17
2. Adoption and Life Before	24
3. Samson's Sunset	53
4. What to Do When the End Is Near	105
5. More of the Magic, Please!	122
6. Dealing with Grief and Guilt	138
7. What to Do After Your Pet Passes	151
8. Letters to Samson	167
Appendices	191
About the Author	238

INTRODUCTION

Hello. My name is Gale. I'm an animal lover, a dog mom, and a recent inductee into the large group of people who have lost a pet they love dearly. While I'm not a licensed grief expert, I do feel compelled to share my story, and my Samson's story, to help other people. Samson was a healing dog and a teacher, which will become evident as you read his story. He would want me to tell you in these first pages that he's thinking about you and your pet, wherever you both are in your story. I echo his sentiments and want to share a message with each of you who find yourself reading this book.

1. This book is written for pet parents who have just received a diagnosis that their dog or cat (or any animal, but for simplicity, I use "pet" throughout the book) has a life-threatening condition. It could be cancer, heart disease, one of many kidney or liver conditions, or even just general failing health. A bleak prognosis of weeks to months has been thrust upon you, in what often feels like a shock because your pet seemed fine just days before you learned the awful news.

If this is you, I am so sorry you've begun this part of your journey, as I wish you had so much more time with your beloved pet. I hope you find some comfort and assistance in our story, but sadly these pages don't hold the answers to stop the inevitable. My heart goes out to you, your pet, and your family.

2. This book is for pet parents who have just said goodbye to their best friend. Regardless of how they passed, whether by accident, long-term illness, or an unexpected short-term decline as described above, you now face the terrible reality that you'll never be greeted by your sweet boy or girl when you walk in the door, you can't hug them ever again, and there is an incredibly big hole in your heart.

If this is you, I mourn for you and for your pet who is no longer living on this earth. I don't have words to adequately describe the difficulty you face. I'm sitting in the midst of it myself as I type this, and it's truly one of the worst things in the world. Pets are pure unconditional love, and your grief is valid. I will be open about my own grieving process throughout this book, with the hope that it may be helpful to you.

3. To some extent, this book may be a resource for new pet parents who want a very early glimpse into what to expect at the end of their pet's life. I think back to 2017 when I adopted Samson, my first dog as an adult. I did so many things right, but now that I've been through literally everything with my first pet, I believe some of the insights in this book would have been very helpful for me to know early on. While I offer suggestions for what pet parents could try at the very end of their pet's life, I wish I'd done some of it in the earlier years as well. I think it would have eased my pain here at the end of my beautiful journey with Samson.

4. Finally, I believe this book may be a nice resource for friends and family members of those grieving the loss of a pet. An early reader of this book thanked me and said, "I don't have any dogs or cats, but I finally understand why some people I've known have had such a tough time losing a pet." If this is you, thank you for seeking to understand and for helping your loved one through their grieving process.

Samson's Story shares the journey of one dog, with guest appearances by many of the people and pets he loved most. I will be candid about my choices with respect to treatment and care, as some of my story may resonate with your particular experience. In my own search for help, it was hard for me to find specific information about the end-of-life journey for one's pet and how to process the heavy grief, so I want to share as much as I've learned as possible. There are some books and resources to consider if you want more help with treatment options, but that topic isn't covered within this book. A pet who receives a bleak prognosis often does not have many options in terms of fighting a disease or illness. However, there are still things we can do for our pets and for ourselves to make this terrible time a little bit easier.

This book is divided into eight chapters:

Chapter 1: Saying Goodbye—This chapter chronicles the last day of Samson's life. I think it's important to start here, but I've gotten feedback that some people find it too hard to read. If this is you, skip ahead and consider coming back later if it feels right.

Chapter 2: Adoption and Life Before—These pages quickly detail the earlier seasons of Samson's life, so you know more about him and how we got to where we did.

Chapter 3: Samson's Sunset—I share a day-by-day account of the last few weeks of his life to give a real glimpse into what happens, both good and bad.

Chapter 4: What to Do When the End Is Near—These are practical how-tos that can help a pet parent prepare for the end. You might skip to this section if you find the "Saying Goodbye" and "Samson's Sunset" chapters too difficult to read.

Chapter 5: More of the Magic, Please!—This chapter goes deeper into the spiritual side of pet loss.

Chapter 6: Dealing with Grief and Guilt—The two big G's require their own chapter.

Chapter 7: What to Do After Your Pet Passes—This chapter contains more practical how-tos about the days and months after you say goodbye.

Chapter 8: Letters to Samson—I share my personal grieving moments during the three months after losing my boy.

This book also includes the following appendices that are meant to supplement Samson's story:

Appendix 1: Additional Reading—Some books I found helpful for pet end of life and grief care.

Appendix 2: Survey Data Results—Full results of the primary survey data that will be referenced throughout the book.

Appendix 3: Samson's Health Data—Link to a website I created with detailed bloodwork and symptoms Samson experienced in his final six months.

Appendix 4: Checklists for Dos & Don'ts—A set of quick reference guides for things to remember during the final days you have with your pet and what to do after they die.

Appendix 5: Resources for Family & Friends—A helpful guide for friends and family who may need coaching on how to talk about pet death and support friends through the loss of a beloved pet.

Appendix 6: Quality of Life Scale (The HHHHHMM Scale)—A worksheet that pet owners can use to assess their pet's health and quality of life as they near the end.

Appendix 7: Money Spent on Vet, Supplements, Medicine, & Diet During Samson's Sunset—A detailed look at the financial side of Samson's sunset period.

Appendix 8: Samson's Story, which I Read to Him on May 17th—This is the story of Samson's life that I wrote and read to him the day before he passed away.

Appendix 9: More Photos of Samson.

This book is not meant to prescribe anything in terms of treatment or caregiving, and I must include the following disclaimer: I am not a vet of any kind, and this book does not contain medical advice. Samson's Story is also meant to be a very short read, as you have more important things to do right now, especially if your pet is still alive.

I read a book on dog cancer right after Samson's diagnosis, and it was extremely long—I felt like I should read it, but I didn't want to take any time away from being fully present with Samson and my family. My goal is to keep this to a three- to four-hour-long read.

This book references a survey I conducted to get some primary data on pet loss grief. The survey results are based on responses from 121 pet parents, 84 percent of which are dog parents, 14 percent cat parents, and 2 percent other pet parents. Respondents reported that 92 percent of their pets lived to age seven and older, and 69 percent to age 11 or older. Cancer, general old age, complications from medicines or surgeries, liver and kidney disease, and heart disease/attack are the most common causes of pet death, accounting for 77 percent of pet deaths within the survey population. Thank you to all of the survey respondents for sharing their insights and experiences, including those who agreed to be quoted in this book. Complete survey results can be found in Appendix 2.

My professional background is in finance, investment, data, and analysis. While I have built a nearly twenty-year career on one of the most tangible and irrefutable things we have—numbers—I also wholeheartedly believe in that which we cannot touch. I reference magic in the subtitle of the book because these pages contain so many lovely synchronicities and moments that could only be explained by a greater universal force. Samson's story is filled with beautiful moments of magic, and I share them all, hoping that they may open doors for others to see magic in their own pets' stories. This book also references animal communication a number of times. This form of communication is done via telepathy, and while it sounds wild, a few Google searches will surface stories of finding lost pets, fixing terrible behavior problems, and many other "wow moments" with animal communicators using telepathy!

SAMSON'S STORY

I send you my warmest thoughts and healing energy for what you're going through or have just gone through. I began writing this book just five days after saying goodbye to my sweet Samson, who stars in this book as our protagonist and hero. My heart is still raw from the loss. The most important thing for us all to remember throughout the pet loss process is that we are doing everything we can. We are doing everything right. Regardless of the "should haves" we can rattle off, whether from accidents we believe we played a role in, treatments we wish we had or had not done, or other decisions we believe could have made the outcome different, the actual course of history is the result of all of us doing the best we can for our best friends.

Pets are family. They love us unconditionally, and we love them so much too. Anticipatory and post-death grief are very real. In fact, some experts say it may be even harder to lose a pet than some friends or family members. Pets are constant sources of love and joy in our lives, and we owe it to ourselves and to them to take time to reflect on their last days and the healing journey we must go through once they leave us. In case it's helpful to hear more voices to support the notion that pet loss grief is real, consider the following comments from some of the survey respondents:

> "I don't think people realize how tough and devastating it can be until they go through it themselves. It's not just a pet, it's a family member."

> "My pet's death has caused a lot of trauma and shock. It's hard when many in society don't see pet loss as a serious loss that causes a lot of grief."

"It feels like it's harder to miss and grieve an animal than a human. They are the only creatures that show unconditional love. So receiving and losing that is so hard."

"Grieving a pet is a pandemic and not validated nor discussed often enough."

"Employers don't really take the time to be empathetic or compassionate ... but losing a pet can be just as distressing as losing a relative or close friend."

"Losing my dogs has been just as painful as losing my grandmother."

My husband, Matt, always says that our pets deserve to live forever. They are perfect. So much more perfect than we humans. He's right. Their lives are too short. Their lives are many, many years too short. 🖤

Chapter 1

SAYING GOODBYE

It was May 18, 2024. A cool spring morning in Chicago. Samson had a rough time the night before. He was shaking, wouldn't eat, and was finding it hard to drink water and stand up. We slept outside on the back deck so we could be near our boy, making him as comfortable as possible. He loved sleeping outside, which gave him free access to cool breezes and the opportunity to sniff all the good scents wafting by.

At 5:30 AM, Matt and I woke up with the early morning sun and did what we had discussed late the night before. We made some calls and moved his at-home euthanasia appointment from May 20th to today—May 18th. We weren't sure he'd make it to Monday morning, and we knew if he went into distress on a Sunday, our only option would be to let him pass on his own or take him to an emergency vet. This wasn't the right move for us because we have another dog—a two-year-old shepherd mix named Murphy, who adored his big brother. We wanted Murphy to be able to smell Samson's body and know he was gone. And we also didn't want Samson to be in any distress or pain if we waited too long.

We were just sixteen days into the estimated one to two months he was given to live. The day before, I thought I had three sleeps left with him. Waking up on the 18th, there should have been two sleeps left, but that had disintegrated to zero. I had mere hours left with my boy, as our appointment was now locked in for noon.

We took Samson for one last car ride as a family. It was one of his favorite things. He never cared where we went. He was just happy to be in the back seat with the window down, letting the air flap his ears as he sniffed to his heart's content. That morning, Matt and I lifted him into the car like we had for the past four years, with Matt picking up his front legs and me lifting him from the back. He was no longer strong enough to help us with the lift, but we could tell he was happy to be getting into his black Subaru Legacy that he loved so much. We drove to get a coffee and some allergy medicine that I needed at a drugstore. I sat in the backseat with Samson, and Murphy was in the front next to my husband, who drove us. I called my sister and told her to come fast and say goodbye to him. I FaceTimed my friend Renata, who loved Samson, and let her say her final farewell from three states away. I pet his soft fur and long ears, I sang our familiar songs to him, and I reveled in that last car ride with my sweet senior puppy.

We got back home with just 2.5 hours left with him in our lives. My sister arrived, and I let her have some time alone with him to say goodbye. She was with me the day I adopted him nearly seven years ago when he was a spry six- to seven-year-old yellow Labrador. On this day, he was a thirteen- to fourteen-year-old yellow Labrador, and his time had come. He knew it was his time too. He tucked in on my husband, my sister, and me as we took turns loving him. He nuzzled up to us, almost like he knew he was saying "so long" for the last time.

SAMSON'S STORY

My last picture with Samson.

My sister left at 11 a.m. because I wanted just my husband and me to be present for the final hour of Samson's life. Matt and I laid by him and loved him, and loved him, and loved him more. With fifteen minutes to go, Matt walked Murphy over to our neighbor's house and came back alone. He picked Samson up from his bed on the back deck—it would be Matt's last of many, many times picking up our boy, who had suffered from arthritis and hip dysplasia through most of his golden years with us.

Matt laid Samson on his big bed in the living room, which was covered in his favorite white fluffy blanket. I felt like time was slipping away—a freight train was on the tracks, and it was coming for us. There was nothing I could do to stop it. It was terrible, but it was also the right thing to do for him. I had dreaded this moment so many times. You see, I always sang Samson a song before going to bed. It was sung to the tune of the "Good Night, Farewell, Aufwiedersen, Adieu" song from *The Sound of Music*. It's the same tune from the *Ted Lasso* episode where the soccer team performed it for Ted right before he left for the States. I'd sing to Samson, "Good night, my boy, my sweet angelic puppy. Goodnight, my sweet yellow Labrador, gooooooooodddddd niiiiiiiiiigggghhhhht, gooooooooodddddd niiiiiiiiiigggghhhhht, good night." And then I'd tell him "Good night my love, Mommy loves you!" In all those nightly renditions, I knew there would come a time when I'd sing my Samson his final goodnight song. It always hung out there, but I mostly ignored it and focused on the joy singing to him brought me. I had adopted a senior dog, and I never knew exactly how much time I'd have with him. I always knew I just had to enjoy what time I did have. But today was the last day I could sing it while hugging his snuggly body. And that made me weep with sadness.

We kept loving on Samson and talking to him, telling him how much we had loved all the amazing years with him. Then the knock came; the vet had arrived.

Sweet Samson perked up a bit when she entered. He'd always loved having guests, and he wanted to greet her properly. He couldn't quite get up, but he did raise his head and move towards her to say hello. Since we had to move up the appointment by two days, this was a vet we hadn't spoken with yet. Seeing him try to greet her, I asked if we were right—was this really his time? Should we continue with the plan to say goodbye?

The vet explained, "There is a window of time during which euthanasia makes sense. Some dogs still have some energy for things during the window, and others have lost all energy. Even though he's perked up a bit, he is certainly in the window based on what I see."

And I already knew that. But I had to ask. What if I was wrong? What if I was robbing him of time? What if he didn't want to go? Making this decision for a pet is a gift and a curse, all wrapped into one.

The vet explained everything and said she would give him the first shot, which is administered like a vaccine. Matt and I were kneeling by Samson where he could see us, with both of our heads near his face. We kept petting him, telling him how much we loved him. I sang him his goodnight song one last time, gave him some kisses, and we told the vet we were ready.

She gave him the first shot, and his breathing slowed. A soft snore ensued. We continued to stroke his soft fur. Tears were streaming uncontrollably at this point. She checked to make sure he couldn't feel any pain in his paws, and then she told us she would step back and start to prepare the second medicine, which would be administered intravenously.

He was sleeping so peacefully. We hugged him, and then we gave the green light to administer the final medicine that would stop his heart.

It took just about one minute. Samson's breathing slowed further and further. And in an instant, the energy shifted to a lightness I'll never forget. I knew my baby was gone. I felt the energy change the moment his soul left his body. I was comforted that he was no longer in pain, weighed down by the heaviness of his liver cancer and failing body. His whiskers gave one last twitch, which prompted me to kiss him right there. The vet said sometimes electrical charges, especially in their snout, can still fire after they pass. She said, "I like to think it's because they enjoyed smelling good smells so much that it's the last thing to go."

It was so much more peaceful than I had expected. I felt a calm I wasn't expecting. I looked into his eyes, and I knew we had done the right thing for him.

The vet stepped out so we could bring Murphy back home to learn of his brother's passing. This was one of the more difficult moments for me. Murphy ran in with Matt and went straight to his brother's bed to check on him, just like he did every time he entered the house. He gave one quick sniff, paused for half a second, and began to run through the house, hackles up, with a ferocity I've never seen. He intended to seriously harm whoever had done this to his brother. He ran back to Samson's bed, barking and growling. But all of a sudden, he stopped. He slowly looked back and forth a few times at the ceiling above Samson's body. And then he was quiet. He retreated from attack mode and sniffed Samson's body head to tail a few times before he walked away.

I don't know how I missed it, but only Matt saw this happen. We believe Samson's spirit was telling Murphy it would be okay, and that's why he calmed down. The funny thing is I'd had a feeling I should record the exchange, but I didn't have time to get my phone out once Murphy burst through the door. Oh how I wish I'd gotten this exchange on video, but if only one of us was meant to see it, I'm glad it was Matt. I already believed in this sort of thing, but to hear Matt tell the story now is quite something.

I took Murphy back to our neighbor's house so we could help the vet carry Samson's body to her vehicle. She wrapped him up in some clean blankets, covered his sweet face, and moved his body to a stretcher. Matt helped her carry the body out, and we placed him in the back of her SUV amid some faux flowers and battery powered candles. The vet pulled back the blanket covering his head, and I gave him one last kiss.

I asked the vet if it was typical to feel the energy shift like that, as I'd never heard anyone talk about it. She said that some people definitely feel a shift, and she recalled the most curious thing she had ever experienced. "I was helping a family say goodbye to their dog outside, and a huge flock of birds flew out of a nearby tree at the exact moment her heart stopped beating."

My eyes got wide. I had Samson talk with an animal communicator right after he was diagnosed with liver cancer, two weeks ago to the day. One of the things Samson told her was "Death is like a flock of birds. They're there, and then all of a sudden, they're gone." It was a sign from Samson that everything would be okay, and that we had selected the exact right time to say goodbye to him.

Chapter 2

ADOPTION AND LIFE BEFORE

To properly share my experience at the end of Samson's life, I need to go back to the earlier years. I think about life in terms of seasons. There was his adoption season, condo life season, road trip season, Chicago house season, Tennessee cabin season, and then the sunset season, which is the main focus of this book.

I didn't realize until after his passing how distinct each of the seasons were, with the changing of the seasons due to several things: the macroenvironment (like COVID), my choices (like selling my first condo to get away from insufferable neighbors), and Samson's health needs (at one point, it became too hard for him to walk up stairs). Each season has a special place in my heart, even his last one.

Adoption Season and Finding Love

In early 2017, I was living with my dear friend Renata in a West Town condo. We began trading wild bar nights out for dog sitting nights in. In the first half of that year, we probably sat for a dozen dogs, a few of them quite often. In June, the mom of one of our favorites,

Tellulahbelle Grace, told us they were moving from Chicago back to Dallas. And boy did I cry. In that moment, I realized I needed to think about adopting a dog of my own, especially since Renata was about to move out as well.

I grew up with Labs, and one of my favorite dogs I'd watched earlier that year was Penelope, a five-year-old chocolate Lab. I decided to reach out to the Chicagoland Lab Rescue about fostering to adopt. They asked me to go on their website and pick a dog to foster. There were dozens and dozens—how could I pick? Instead, I asked them to find one that needed me. My requests were fairly simple: a senior Lab (seniors are typically defined as three-plus years old and are harder to adopt out), dog friendly, kid friendly, and ready to be picked up in early August.

In mid-July, I was watching Penelope again, and we were in the flower-filled park near my condo. It wasn't an official dog park, but over the years, it had become a favorite neighborhood gathering place for furry friends. A sweet husky pup no more than six months old was frolicking across the park next to his handsome dad. I kept calling this dog Samson even though I knew the puppy's name was Jameson. After this happened three or four times, I noted to myself how weird it was. Despite having a crush on Jameson's dad, I wasn't able to land a date with him, but I did find myself on a date with a friend of a friend a few weeks later. We were standing in line for Jeni's ice cream in Wicker Park. Out of the blue, my date asked a woman in front of us if her dog's name was Samson. Nope. It was Gus. But I had to ask, "Where did you get that name from?" My date said, "I don't know. It just popped into my head." I replied, "So weird, because I keep thinking of that name too." That was our only date, but this exchange made it a memorable one!

At the end of July, I got an email from the team at Chicagoland Lab Rescue. They said, "We found your dog! He's a six- to seven-year-old yellow Lab who is very sweet, loves walks, and needs to be rehomed because his current mom was just diagnosed with cancer. He has a thyroid condition and needs to be on medicine long term. He will be ready to pick up on August 5, and his name is Samson." I about fell out of my chair! The universe had been signaling to me that this would be my dog. In hindsight, there is not a truer truth in my whole life. Samson was absolutely meant to be my dog.

My sister and I went to pick up Samson on August 5 from his last home. He was so sweet, and, without any hesitation, he jumped into the car with us. Little did I know this would be the one and only time he jumped into a car! Despite having lots of health problems right off the bat—allergies, worms, and too high a dose of thyroid medicine—I let the rescue know I had "foster failed" and would be officially adopting Mr. Samson.

My first picture with Samson, when I picked him up from his previous owner's house in August 2017.

Samson loved life with me from the jump. His favorite thing to do was go on walks. He would do a little dance with his front paws, throw his head back and smile so big when he'd get to go outside with his mommy. He had this weird way of pooping where he'd run back and forth a number of times and then do a walking squat while leaving a trail of Easter eggs. Not only did he still poop like a puppy, but he also ran like a puppy. It was more of a lope, akin to what a horse would do. He didn't run often, but when he did, it was pure magic. There was so much love and joy in his being when he did his puppy run to someone.

Right after I adopted him, I noticed he wasn't quite as mobile as other dogs his age. I would later find out he had a very bad case of hip dysplasia, but right after his adoption, I learned something at a work event that I put into motion right away. After telling a colleague I had just adopted a Lab, he shared that his family's Lab was still living at sixteen! He said she'd had some bad mobility challenges around age eleven, and the vet had suggested a trifecta of fish oil, Dasuquin (a joint health supplement), and Carprofen (a nonsteroidal anti-inflammatory drug). He said it changed his dog's life, and she bounced back wonderfully. Wow! I started Samson on fish oil and Dasuquin right away, as my research indicated those supplements would help his joints from deteriorating as quickly. He took them twice a day for the rest of his life, and we added in Carprofen when he was about ten or eleven years old. I look back on this moment as one that likely gave me many more good months or even years with my sweet boy. A divine nudge from the universe for which I am so grateful.

Samson loved meeting other dogs and people. Despite his hip dysplasia, he'd come alive around other dogs—dancing, jumping, and even displaying his goofy version of a downward dog pose when playing with other pups. He had an energy about him that attracted wonderful things. I'd been looking for love for years, and I'm not at all surprised that I met my husband, Matt, just three months after Samson came into my life.

Not only did I find romantic love because of Samson, but I learned what unconditional love was. Samson was the first being who loved me for me. No judgment, no conditions, no negativity. I was sorting through some old trauma I'd started to remember in my mid-thirties, just a few weeks before Samson came into my life. Lo and behold, Samson's adoption season coincided beautifully with the beginning of my healing journey. The saying in the dog rescue world is so accurate: Who Saved Who? I am forever grateful to Samson for loving me during a hard season in my own life and for teaching me what unconditional love looks like.

Samson getting into some old-fashioned puppy trouble in his first home!

Moving In with Daddy

I loved my first condo, and Samson did too for the first ten months of his life with me. But my neighbors were not cut from the same cloth as my future neighbors, who are amazing and beautiful souls. I am now grateful to those jerky neighbors for sending us packing, as we found a great condo a few blocks west with a killer view of the Chicago skyline. This was Samson's second residence with me and where he would spend two and a half years of his life.

The condo Matt bought was lovely—a small, top-floor, two-bed, two-bath in a three-unit building. Samson loved jumping up on our big gray couch and twisting his body each and every way during a good nap. He liked to hang his head off the couch, resting it on the windowsill to watch people outside walking by. He was always excited to go to the back deck and sit on the comfy double chaise lounge and enjoy a nice breeze on a cool Chicago day.

Samson loved to nap on his gray couch.

Samson getting some outdoor time on his double chaise lounger.

While we no longer had a park a block away, we'd take advantage of lazy weekend mornings to take a long walk to get coffee and go to one of two larger parks where other dogs liked to play. Samson would walk for hours and hours during this time of his life. He loved to accompany Matt and me to patios, bars, and friends' houses. It was during this season with us that I think he finally realized he was home. I was his third mom, and after our first couple of years, he was settling into the idea that I'd stick by his side. He'd be so happy that sometimes he'd throw his head back and go "woo woo." It was part bark, part holler, and all joy. When he was especially happy, he'd add a jump with each woo woo exclamation. It was so unique that some of our friends and even random people in the dog park started calling him Woo Woo.

Samson hated his raincoat, but he loved his walks!

Samson also loved it when company visited us at the condo. After greeting them on the street, he'd be the first up the front entryway stairs, and he'd stop at the landing on the second floor to check that everyone in our party was accounted for. Then he'd trot up the last half of the stairs with a smile.

Samson welcomed many of his dog friends for visits at our condo. He also accompanied Matt and me on a number of road trips. We realized he was an excellent traveler in the car, and we loved having him join us on excursions to southern Illinois for a cabin retreat, Pittsburgh for his Aunt Caitlin's birthday, Delaware to see Aunt Tracy and Uncle Ed, and Rhode Island for Christmas with Grandma and Grandpa. Samson also joined us on our wedding day and came with us to Lanesboro, Minnesota, for a laid-back honeymoon. The week in Lanesboro remains one of my favorite times with Samson; he went everywhere with us—on long hikes, to art galleries, outdoor patios, and even the tennis courts. He jumped into a lake trying to catch some ducks on this trip, and I was lucky enough to catch this hilarious memory on video.

Samson took a hike with us in Lanesboro, MN, during our honeymoon.

At the beach in Rehoboth, DE, while visiting Aunt Tracy.

Meeting goats for the first time in southern Illinois. Samson loved all animals!

One of my favorite memories of Samson in the condo is how much the two little kids on the first floor loved him. They would squeal with joy when they ran into him coming in and out for his walks. Leila was two, and she'd hug Samson hard and not let go until her mom pried her away. Leila's brother Cooper was four, and one time he showed us his yellow, stuffed dog he'd proudly named Jamson. My heart! Our sweet Samson had made such an impression on even these young kiddos. How lucky we were to have him in our life.

Road Trip!

Around the age of ten, Samson was starting to struggle with the stairs leading up to the third-floor condo. We knew he needed ground floor living ASAP, so we found a fixer-upper home a bit further north in Chicago. Divine timing had us close on the house one week before the city shut down due to COVID. We found a general contractor, secured a construction loan, and put all plans in place for the rehab. We tried to sell our West Town condo, but no one was interested in buying small condos when we were all stuck inside due to COVID in 2020.

So we decided to roll the dice on renting the condo and traveling during the house remodel. In hindsight, this was a crazy decision. Most homeowners would want to be nearby during a major renovation. Traveling did make things tricky, but I am so glad we did it anyway. In October 2020, we traded Matt's two-door green jeep in for a boring yet reliable black Subaru Legacy sedan (which I now call Samson's car), packed that thing with as much as she could hold, and then headed off for a three-month trip across fifteen states.

I'm not sure if Samson took any trips with his first and second set of parents, but he got to live what our friend Mike calls an "elite life" with us. He rode through a lake town in a golf cart in the Ozarks. He woo wooed at horses in Arkansas and Tennessee. He chased a deer through a forest and hunted his first armadillo in Texas. He put his paws in the ocean in Delaware and Massachusetts. He visited some of his favorite people—Grandma and Grandpa in Rhode Island, Uncle Jeff in Virginia, Aunt Tracy in Delaware, and many more.

Samson in 18 inches of snow in the Catskills, New York.

Samson at an old dude ranch in Texas.

Hiking in Austin.

A cold beach day in Massachusetts.

SAMSON'S STORY

Samson's favorite part of the road trip was sticking his face out the window like this.

Matt and I became expert packers during this season. We stayed in each Airbnb for one to five days, so there was a lot of packing and unpacking. We measured days in "sleeps," and we'd tell Samson how many sleeps we had left at each spot. Once we got to zero sleeps, Samson was on alert. During the packing process, he made sure to sit right by the car so he didn't get left behind. Each time, we'd reassure him he was coming with, and we'd tell him he was the "most precious-est" of the cargo we had. Our final step was lifting him into the back seat atop his bed and blanket and buckling his harness. You could sense his relief and joy when we started rolling down the road with the windows open—he'd made it in with his people and was ready for the next adventure!

Samson's House in Chicago (2021-2024)

After three months on the road, we spent another few months in various Airbnbs not too far from our new house as they finished the gut rehab. We were able to move in during April 2021. Our new home was a Jefferson Park bungalow—a 1919 brick beauty with six stairs up to the first floor. Samson wasn't loving even this small number of stairs, and I was worried he had developed a fear of them after months on the road where he didn't have to worry about stairs most of the time. After posting in some Facebook groups to see if anyone had tips, we realized it might be pain, not fear, that was causing Samson's hesitancy to take even a few steps. I explained to the vet he was having trouble with the stairs, and she suggested we X-ray his hips. I will never forget bursting into tears of guilt when the vet relayed that Samson's X-rays confirmed he had a very bad case of hip dysplasia. My sweet boy had likely been battling pain for quite some time, and we didn't know. We started him on Carprofen right away and hired someone to build a wooden ramp up to our back deck so that Samson could come and go on his own.

The new neighborhood was idyllic. Tree-lined streets, beautiful old four-square homes and brick bungalows, and lots of lovely neighbors and friendly dogs. Our street didn't get much through traffic, so Samson often liked to lie on the front lawn and greet passersby. He'd mosey over to the neighbors to visit with his fellow senior dog friend, Jackson, a big, fluffy, black bear of a dog who was just as friendly and mellow as our Samson.

Samson hanging out in the front yard.

We'd often walk Samson to the nearby park and let him run around off leash with his dog friends. So many woo woos were had. We took car trips to the dog beach in Chicago, Matt's favorite coffee shops,

SAMSON'S STORY

and special dog parks to meet up with his furry friends. Samson was in pretty good health these years, except for intermittent limps and minor mobility issues. He also started having some nerve pain in his legs and was prescribed Gabapentin, which really helped him.

I knew we were squarely in his senior years at this point, and he was now probably eleven, which is the average life expectancy of a Labrador. I began taking Samson to the vet every six months for bloodwork, and Matt and I started talking about getting a puppy before Samson was too much older. We started fostering dogs to get used to the idea of having a second, and we were able to help Lucy Linna, Dolly, Duke, Ellie, Ember, and Midnight find their forever homes.

Lucy Linna, one of our foster dogs, sticking close to Samson at the top of his ramp.

Samson and fosters Duke and Ellie on their way to the dog park.

Just like I'd heard Samson's name before I found him, I had been hearing the name Murphy for over a year, ever since we met another yellow lab named Murphy in the Ozarks on our road trip. So we knew we were looking for a puppy named Murphy. Based on other insights from animal communicators I'd spoken with, we were looking for a black and tan male that would be in a litter of pups north of the city, just after Christmastime. Samson had taught me that the universe will give me signs when I am supposed to find a dog, and that time was getting close!

Sure enough, I found Murphy on PetFinder in early 2022. He was a cute little German Shepherd and cattle dog mix. We did another foster to adopt and failed quite quickly. Murphy joined our family when he was eight weeks old and just nine pounds of puppy cuteness. We'd fostered a handful of dogs before Murphy, all of whom loved to lie by Samson. Murphy was no different; he adored his big brother Samson. Murphy learned quickly that Samson didn't play like other dogs, but that didn't matter—Murphy often took one of his stuffed toys or antlers and laid by Samson while he chewed it. Sometimes he would lie on the bed with Samson, sometimes on top of Samson, and as he got bigger and bigger, on the floor right next to Samson's bed.

Murphy loved being right by his brother Samson from day one!

SAMSON'S STORY

When Murphy joined our party of three, Samson was walking with a limp. To our amazement, he really perked up upon Murphy's arrival. Even though he didn't outwardly love Murphy like Murphy loved him, Samson certainly found more joy in life when he could share his favorite things with his brother. More dog parks, beach trips, coffee runs, long walks, and road trips were enjoyed by the whole family.

One of our road trips with the boys was to the north woods of Georgia for my fortieth birthday. I rented three cabins and invited lots of friends to join us. After an amazing long weekend, we took our time on the drive back to Chicago, stopping at a handful of Airbnbs over the next month. We had done a cycle of IVF in the summer and planned to implant an embryo after this birthday trip. We weren't successful in getting a healthy embryo per PGT testing, so we decided to shift gears and embrace a kid-free lifestyle with the purchase of a snowbird property. We used this month-long trip to check out various places in Tennessee that we might like, starting in Chattanooga, then Knoxville, and finally around Nashville.

Hiking in Georgia with an assist from Daddy and saying hello to a mule in Tennessee!

It was a lovely road trip with the boys—lots of outside time, hikes, and dog parks. We ultimately decided to look for property within an hour of Nashville, which was our favorite spot of the bunch and also the closest to Chicago. We headed back home and started the search for five acres on a river or lake that was within our budget. Exactly two months later, I found the perfect property on Zillow. It was an old farm on a river that had been divided into five-acre lots. I flew down to see it, and it was definitely "the one." We were under contract to buy it the very next day. Matt and I started researching how to prep the site and build a cabin.

Around this time, Samson had a mid-grade mast cell tumor removed from his inner ear. On one of his many vet visits, I'd pointed out eight or nine lumps and bumps for the vet to check out. She knew right away this one in his ear looked concerning, and a biopsy confirmed we should remove the cancerous cells. The surgery was a success, and subsequent tests showed that he had recovered fully. I started taking Samson to acupuncture to try and help ease his joint pain. He seemed to like it, so we went every few weeks while still in Chicago.

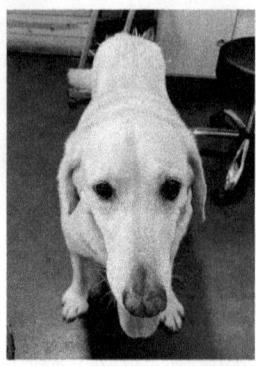

Samson at an acupuncture treatment.

Now that he was twelve years old, I was starting to worry about him more and more. The anticipatory loss of a pet is a terrible thing, and it started to rear its ugly head for me around this time. I so badly wanted Samson to be able to spend time on the new property we just bought. I knew we would keep the land for our own retirement and sunset season, and I desperately hoped my baby boy would be part of my memories on this land that already felt sacred to me.

Cabin in Tennessee!

We drove the boys down to see the property in February 2023. I took lots of pictures and videos and was so thankful Samson at least got to be there for a few amazing days. But, what if I could get a small house built ASAP? I researched prefabbed cabins and found a company in Kentucky that seemed to be a great option. Early that summer, we ordered the largest prefab Amish-built cabin they could legally put on the road, and we began the site prep for tree removal, utilities, and a basement foundation.

Samson's first visit to our Tennessee property.

It was a lot of work to manage the cabin build from Chicago, so Matt and I took turns flying to Nashville to ensure things were moving along. Meanwhile, life was pretty much the same for the boys back in Chicago. Murphy went to daycare and training every day, and Samson enjoyed lots of back-deck time, neighborhood strolls, and visits to the nearby park. We started having more health scares with him in late 2023. One time, I came home from a trip to Nashville, and he was walking in tight circles in the backyard. I was beside myself and convinced he'd had a stroke, and that this was it.

A trip to the emergency vet revealed it was vestibular disease, a vertigo-like condition in dogs. Samson had a few recurring vestibular episodes in the following months, and we also noticed increased panting and restlessness. We tested him for Addison's disease and Cushing's disease, the results for which were both negative. His bloodwork was all within the normal ranges, and an ultrasound showed that his organs were fine save for a few small kidney stones. The vet said he likely had GOLPP (geriatric onset laryngeal paralysis and polyneuropathy), a condition similar to ALS in humans, in which a dog finds it harder to walk and harder to swallow. The vet said there was not much we could do other than manage any associated pain—so we increased his dose of Gabapentin as needed and continued his acupuncture, which seemed to work pretty well.

This all happened just as our cabin build was finishing up. The vet had suggested we get another ultrasound, which we booked for a few weeks out at a vet in Tennessee. We packed up Samson's car and left on Christmas Eve 2023 for our first winter in the cabin. I remember being so grateful when we arrived in the wee hours of Christmas morning because my big yellow boy was with us. He had made it long enough to enjoy life in the cabin with his family.

Our first morning in the cabin, Christmas Day 2023.

And enjoy it he did! The winter weather was perfect—not too hot, not too cold, and lots of sunshine. Our small log cabin had a large back deck that overlooked a thick line of trees, behind which the sun set in an array of marvelous hues each evening. We left the sliding door to the back deck open most days so Samson could catch a breeze whenever he liked. We often took the boys back to the creek at the edge of our property. Samson loved to walk into the calm creek water up to his belly, and Murphy enjoyed running about in the shallow water and checking out all the good smells along the shoreline. Matt loved the nights that got cold enough to make a fire in the wood stove, and honestly, the boys seemed so happy to just be in this beautiful place with their mommy and daddy.

Four weeks after we arrived, Samson had the ultrasound that we'd scheduled. The report came back with a clean bill of health. Phew! But just a few days later, he wasn't walking well at all. It was the worst limp we'd seen on him. I started kicking myself for not thinking about a total hip replacement back when Samson was ten or eleven when we'd first learned of his hip dysplasia. I hadn't even thought about the possibility of Samson not being able to walk at all! He loved his mobility so much—what could I do for him?

I ordered Samson a royal blue Walkin' Wheels wheelchair and started researching vets who work on hips. There was only one option in the state of Tennessee— a board-certified veterinary specialist located in Chattanooga. We booked a consult and took Samson there in mid-February. While driving the three hours to the appointment, Matt and I discussed what we should do if Samson was deemed a good candidate for surgery. I was wringing my hands—he was probably thirteen by now, and that seemed quite old for a dog to undergo surgery. However, it was so hard for him to walk at this point that we decided we'd do it, as he might have a few good years of life ahead to enjoy a new hip. We just had to see what the doctor recommended after the exam and go from there.

Samson testing out his wheelchair.

A total hip replacement is a major surgery, and only very healthy dogs should undergo one. The vet's team ran all kinds of tests on Samson, and we learned he was a great candidate for the surgery. I really liked the doctor, who had performed many of these surgeries over the years. His failure rate was 6 percent, and he said he could fix the problem half of the time. So we were given a clean bill of health and a green light from their surgical team, and we were looking at a 97 percent chance that Samson would live through the surgery. They assured us his age was not an issue, as the health of the dog is the primary factor.

At that point, we were leaning towards the surgery. We told them we'd get back to them ASAP with our decision. They brought Samson out of the back room where he'd been sedated for the hip X-rays. We were walking towards our car to start the long trek home when he suddenly collapsed in the parking lot. Luckily, another vet was sitting outside on a break and came to help us. She said his heart rate was quite weak, so they took him back inside on a stretcher.

This was probably one of the worst moments of my life as Samson's mom. What had I just done? What if he dies today? After the longest thirty minutes of my life, they came to tell us Samson would be okay. He'd had some issues with the sedation, including arrhythmia and a failed reversal of one of the two anesthesia drugs used. After another thirty minutes, they let us take him home.

That night, we decided he wouldn't be able to undergo anesthesia in the future, as it was just too hard on his body. So no surgery. But, thankfully, we just got a clean bill of health from all of these tests, so I took comfort in knowing I'd have a lot more good time with him.

In mid-February, I booked an animal communication session with a woman named Mary Helen Schmidt (her website is https://www.itsmynature-mhs.com), whose name I'd recently found when reviewing a pet care business that had been sent to me as a possible investment. It was an hour-long session in which she connected telepathically with Samson and then with Murphy while I was on the phone with her. Even though I'm an amateur animal communicator myself, I find it's hard to connect with my own pets because I know them so well. So I've often booked meetings with other communicators when looking for insights into how my dogs are doing and feeling.

The first question I asked was, "Is Samson happy, and how is he feeling?" Mary Helen said she heard the word "source." Samson told her he didn't feel like a yellow Lab. She could sense he was very loving; she said, "He has been a teacher. He is your teacher, and he takes that role very seriously. It's one of the reasons why he came. He is saying he helps you find your way, and his being here with you is in the big picture. There's so much more to him than meets the eye."

Next, Mary Helen focused on body-level energy to find out how Samson was feeling. She said, "I sense that he hobbles a bit. He has backend stiffness. He takes smaller steps because he doesn't have the stretch of someone who is younger or taller; it's like he has a rubber band between his feet and is constrained in how far he can move." Wow, I thought—that is exactly how he walks!

Mary Helen asked Samson to show her another part of his body. He mentioned that something with his urinary system was not quite right, and the tail area felt very stiff. Mary Helen could tell the energy didn't flow as well in that part of Samson's body. She reminded me that she just describes and doesn't prescribe (which is the case for all animal communicators), and she suggested that acupuncture or a chiropractor adjustment might help to release some of the stuck energy in that area. Reiki and shamanic work were other options. Samson told Mary Helen that he loved massages on his upper body, particularly his shoulders and neck. Very true! But he reiterated that massage on his lower body wouldn't feel good at all.

Sometimes in animal communication sessions, dogs start to ramble on about things they aren't asked about but that are highly interesting and often a window into their soul journey. In this particular session, Samson mentioned that he was a dog of service. He went on to say, "Some dogs give all they can and get cancer. That is okay. They are using their energy for good, which is an output. Sometimes that output causes a deficit." He said, "Dogs would keep doing it over and over and over again, and sometimes it just depletes them of energy. Right now, we don't have any way to help as science hasn't caught up with energy medicine."

Mary Helen reminded me she was paraphrasing the feelings, images, and words that were coming to her from Samson in the session. She told me, "It feels like there are some people you connect with and are sharing Samson and his wisdom to help those people. Samson said he loves to be of service and that this work is very important for your evolution and for his evolution."

I asked if Samson had been with me in a past life. His dry humor surfaced when he told Mary Helen, "Duh," and she couldn't help but chuckle. (This is a common reaction from all of the animal communicators who have talked with Samson—they find him to be quite funny and sarcastic in addition to sweet and loving). Mary Helen sensed that Samson had been with me previously in this life and was an animal my family was really frustrated by and didn't know what to do with. Upon reflection, I told her there had been a coon hound that my parents had for a few months, and he was wild. So wild that at one point I never saw him again, and I was too young to ask what happened to him.

Samson went on to use this as a teaching point. He said, "I was an animal with issues, and you humans couldn't figure it out. But look at things like a deck of cards. It's still just a card, even if it's not the card you wanted. Think of a heart and a spade—a spade is an upside-down heart, so it's two sides of the same coin. Reincarnation can be light and dark."

Mary Helen said she felt a male presence in our house, and I confirmed it was my husband. She said, "Samson is here to help open your husband's heart. I feel like it's very hard for your husband to trust, and Samson shows me it is one of his talents to help with trust."

She said, "I sense Samson has a stomachache. Perhaps a compulsion to get into things he shouldn't get into. When he does it, he does it well and has fun. He is saying that he has to try and experience these things." Samson's left hip surfaced as an issue. Mary Helen said her hand bent all of a sudden and felt like she was trying to smooth the edge of his hip joint. "It feels like lots of scratchy points on the inside of the hip. I am smoothing that with energy work right now."

I asked about the hip replacement to make sure we were making the right decision. He told Mary Helen, "Oh I don't know. I like being home. I feel like I have to keep an eye on Murphy because he is a mess. I don't like going far away from home, and I hate to be away from family."

I also asked if he preferred Chicago or Tennessee life. Mary Helen said, "He loves it in Tennessee and says it is quieter, except for the dogs that howl and bark. He can definitely still hear, though he may be hard of hearing a bit, and he says something is always making a ruckus. It could be that Murphy is barking at owls, vultures, or crows. Ultimately, Samson likes to be wherever you all are. But it makes him really stiff to travel. He doesn't mind either place, though he says there is a little more help with the mobility issues in Chicago. He shows me himself sprawling out, and that feels really good to him. When he's in a vehicle for a long time, he is a bit more nervous, and the turns he does in the seat are very difficult for him." All very true—Murphy is always barking at turkey vultures, and Samson definitely had trouble turning around in the car by that time.

I wanted to know if the wheelchair we had bought for him was helpful. Mary Helen said Samson called it a "contraption." She continued, "He said it's okay, but it's a bit of a challenge to get into. Even though it hurts him to get in and out of it, he does like the freedom it offers. But his freedom isn't dependent on the wheelchair. It's more about doing whatever you need to manage his pain. When he can be still, he is at his very best. He likes to do his work from where he is comfy, which is his fluffy bed. He wants you to know that he thinks of his bed as his place of power right now."

Mary Helen shared, "There is a part of him that doesn't have that joyful, loving energy. This will probably help you know where he's at. If you are okay with lugging him around and helping him with his mobility, he is okay with that. He just wants to stay comfortable. And I don't get that a surgery would fix his mobility."

Mary Helen's last point related to Samson was, "Do you write? Does your husband write? He shows me words. It's in the words. He says it's all there." And then she told Samson she was switching to Murphy, and Samson made her chuckle again as he rolled his eyes.

A few weeks later, I had another animal communicator named Jaime Breeze talk with Samson, this time via Zoom (Jaime's website is https://jaimebreeze.com). The session was similar—Jaime smiled as she said he was a self-proclaimed love bug. She relayed that he enjoyed watching birds out on the deck, and his hips and lower back were hurting him. He showed her his restless leg syndrome and said he was feeling anxious and annoyed by the movement, though it didn't hurt. Jaime saw mushrooms twice during the reading and told me I should try those. Samson also mentioned he wanted to try water therapy.

I wanted to know how I could better communicate with Samson. Jaime said, "He showed me the deck he lies on, and he wants you to sit by him and just feel the wind, the trees, and the sun. Feel the nature, and he is guiding you and teaching you to go deeper and to be able to feel. By doing that, he is going to show you how easy it is. Your first step is to sit with him on the sunny deck and listen and sense everything. He said any sort of creative thing you do—such as painting or drawing—is going to help tap into the right side of the brain and help you feel the deeper connection. He showed me how to visualize his face in your third eye when you are trying to communicate with him. He says, 'Mom, it's so easy and you are already doing it. You're just not trusting enough.'"

We'd had access to acupuncture in Chicago, but not where we lived in Tennessee, so we found a nearby vet who did a lot of physical therapy with dogs. We started booking regular treatments, including laser therapy, shockwave therapy, and hydrotherapy. He regained a lot of his mobility, and while he wasn't loping like a puppy much by this point, he was able to walk on his own and come and go as he wished. We had kept Samson in mind when designing the cabin. It was two floors, with the main floor having a ramp to the front door and the basement level a walk-out so he could come right in on his own. Samson didn't love the gravel driveway and the pasture grass, as he found it uncomfortable and spikey under his paws. In March, we ordered a bunch of sod so he could have a proper lawn and a softer surface during his time outside. He loved lying outside on his new grass! Every Monday, Wednesday, and Friday, Murphy went to doggie day care on the Magic Dog Bus. Yes, it's a school bus for dogs, and it's definitely worth a follow on Facebook or Instagram! The bus would pick Murphy up between 6:00 and 7:00 a.m., and Samson would always join Murphy, Matt, and me as we waited on the front stoop for the bus to pull into our driveway and swing open its double doors for Murph to run on. I could tell Samson was itching to join his brother on the bus, so I booked Samson two field trips on the Magic Dog Bus in April. The gals who run it let me ride along with Murph and Samson, and these are now some of my most cherished memories of Samson's cabin season. He loved being on the bus and meeting the other dogs we picked up along the way. After we dropped off his brother at daycare, they drove us to the local coffee shop where we helped Samson down from the bus and let him enjoy a pup cup treat. Matt collected us from the coffee shop in Samson's car and drove us home, where Samson would resume his normal activities of soaking up sunshine and breezes from a variety of spots on the deck and in the backyard.

Samson thoroughly enjoying a ride on the Magic Dog Bus.

Our last two months at the cabin were great. Quite a few friends visited, and we enjoyed every minute of it. Although I know he loved being at the cabin, I could tell Samson was bored. Some days, he'd sit by the car, hoping to go on mini adventures. Much of the time, we complied, taking him on trips to Lowe's, the town square, or a nearby park. I knew how much Samson loved to see people, and I could sense he wanted to get back to Chicago, where people were more likely to pet him and say hello more often. I was also excited for him to have soft grass and smooth sidewalks everywhere we went in Chicago, which would be a nice break for him from the gravel and pasture grass!

Samson and Murphy enjoying life at the cabin.

Samson enjoyed his therapy sessions, which we continued regularly during our last two months in Tennessee. The vet and vet techs who worked with him all came out to see him off after his last appointment on April 26, two days before we headed back to Chicago for the summer. I was so touched by how much they all loved him. And little did any of us know, it wasn't just his last therapy visit of the season, but it would also be the last therapy visit of his life.

Chapter 3

SAMSON'S SUNSET

We drove back to Chicago on April 28. Matt and I noticed Samson seemed uncomfortable during the eight-hour journey, lying with his front legs straight out, in a kind of superman pose. We stopped at a Wendy's for a bathroom break and dog walk, and I was a bit concerned when Samson abruptly laid down during our short walk. With these concerns plus what we assumed was an anal gland issue, which we also noticed on our drive home, I called the vet the next day. At first, they said they had nothing available all week, but then the receptionist put me on hold and came back to let me know they just had a cancellation, and that I should come in right now. Matt and I lifted Samson into the car, and I drove him straight to the vet.

It had been almost three months since his last bloodwork and ultrasounds, and I had gotten into the habit over the past two years of doing his blood panel every three months (I had been doing it every six months) so that we could catch any health issues early. We asked the vet to clean his anal gland and do the senior bloodwork. I also told the vet that Samson hadn't been eating normally for the past few months. We had assumed he was getting pickier with age, as he'd trained us into making him boiled chicken, rather than giving him kibble or his raw food.

After the exam, the vet reported that Samson's spleen felt enlarged and that some of the liver and kidney values on his bloodwork were high. He suggested we come in and do an ultrasound in three days when he had an available appointment. We went about our normal lives over the next few days, until things took a turn for the worse on May 2.

Thursday, May 2nd

We took Samson into the vet at 8 a.m., fasted, for his tests. We still hadn't received a call by 1 p.m., so Matt and I drove to the vet to check on him. I was starting to worry. Just as we were pulling up and parking, my phone rang. The vet told us we should come in to discuss what was going on. They took us to a room, and the vet showed us Samson's ultrasound, which picked up masses on his liver and damage to his spleen. They had also tested his bile acids and re-tested his liver enzymes, all of which were quite high.

The vet said we were potentially looking at cancer or liver disease. We had two options to diagnose the problem: we could do a needle aspirate cytology to see what type of cells they were, or we could do a biopsy, which would require sedation. Based on the vet's opinion, if we wanted to biopsy, we should also elect to remove the spleen and any operable masses from the liver while sedated.

We were devastated. We had just learned two and a half months ago that Samson didn't do well with anesthesia. And we were so shocked that he went from a clean bill of health to what sounded like a very sick liver in seventy-five days. We asked the vet what he would do. He said if it were his dog, he would start with the cytology. He warned us it's not 100 percent accurate, but it was the best non-invasive option we had.

We told him to do the cytology. And then we waited. And waited. And waited. Nearly two hours later, the doctor came back, and I knew it wasn't good since it had taken so long. He said it was carcinoma. The one we didn't want to see. He turned off the lights and showed us the cytology images from Samson's liver and spleen. He said the foamy looking cells were carcinoma, and the spleen was trying to act like a lymph node and clean the liver. But the spleen had started bleeding and was essentially attacking itself.

My heart dropped. I asked how much time Samson had. He said, "based on his liver and bile acid levels, I would say one month." My world stopped, and I fell into one of the two plastic chairs in the exam room. I just couldn't believe it. We were utterly devastated.

The vet suggested we get a second opinion. He said we could also consider surgery. We again asked what he would do if it was his pet. He said, "Honestly, I would take him home, keep him as comfortable as possible, and enjoy the time I have left with him."

In hindsight, this was the right and best answer. In that moment, I wasn't quite ready to hear it. We went home, and I called my sister and told her Samson has cancer and that she should come see him soon. I called my good friend Peggy and told her the same. I started doing research. I emailed Samson's vet from Tennessee the pictures of his cytology results and bloodwork to get a second opinion. I cried.

And I cried.

When I was done crying, I felt like I should do something. So I started reading the *Dog Cancer Survival Guide* to learn about food and how I could try to help Samson by giving him the healthiest diet possible. I made a list of what was both safe for dogs and high in antioxidants. Matt went to the store and bought beets, carrots, bell peppers, broccoli, green beans, peas, spinach, purple sweet potatoes, organic turmeric powder, cold pressed coconut oil, chicken breast, chicken broth, brown rice, and milk thistle. He couldn't find the omega-3 fatty acids in liquid form that were supposedly good to add to a cancer-fighting diet. It was late, and Aunt Peggy was coming over to see Samson, so we put the groceries away and cracked open beers with our friend. We all cried together, both for Samson and for Peggy's dog Aksel, who had died a few years earlier from bone cancer. Our hearts were raw. What were we going to do without our Woo Woo boy?

Friday, May 3rd

It was Friday. Garbage day. Samson's favorite day of the week. The garbage collector has to back up into our alley because of the narrow street entrances. For the past few years, Samson would hear the "beep beep beep" of the truck and rush to the backyard. Tail wagging, he'd wait for Mr. Bobby to throw Milk-Bones over the fence and eat as many as we'd let him. Today was no different for Samson, though it felt very different for me. We heard the beep beep beep of the truck, and I took him outside. He moseyed down his ramp and waited in the yard for his bones. We had been gone the last four months in Tennessee, so Mr. Bobby was very glad to see his buddy Samson. He stopped the truck by our backyard, turned it off, and yelled, "Saaaammmmmsssoooooonnnnn" just like always. He threw a few bones. I turned off my phone's video that had been capturing this moment, opened our back gate, and went out to the alley. I couldn't keep the tears from falling down my face. I looked up at Bob sitting in his big baby blue garbage truck, and I could barely get it out. "He's got cancer, Bob. You better come see him." Bob's face fell. He got out of the truck and followed me into the yard. He said, "You know, I've been thinking about Samson and just had a feeling he might not be okay when you got back." Bob loves to hand out dog treats on his routes, and I know Samson had always been one of his favorites. Seeing how much this big burly garbage collector loved Samson was both comforting and gut wrenching.

Old pictures of Samson waiting for Milk-Bones to launch over the fence from Mr. Bobby.

The Tennessee vet got back to me right away. She confirmed it was likely an aggressive cancer based on the cytology images, and she suggested I take Samson to a veterinarian oncologist. I told her I'd already made an appointment at the one nearby our house, but the soonest time available was two weeks out. She inspired me to try calling a few more vets, and I was able to find one with an opening on Tuesday, May 7, five days post diagnosis. I wanted to ask about a drug called Sorafenib that I'd just found in my research. I also ordered some functional mushrooms and liver defense powder online. It felt good to do something tangible while swimming in a massive sea of uncertainty.

I sent a note to my team to let them know the sad news:

> Hi All - Samson was unfortunately diagnosed with liver cancer yesterday so I will be trying to take as much time off with him as I can in the coming weeks. I'm still in a bit of shock as he was given just a month to live. I hope the doctor was wrong, but I suppose it's time for me to get prepared for what will be coming. Please hug all of your pets for me and my sweet yellow boy.

Finally, I reached out to Mary Helen and Jaime, the two animal communicators Samson had spoken with in the past few months. I looked back at my notes from each of those conversations, and my heart dropped when I read the notes from Mary Helen's call a few months ago in which Samson actually talked about cancer.

> Samson mentioned he was a dog of service. He went on to say, "Some dogs give all they can and get cancer. That is okay. They are using their energy for good, which is an output. Sometimes that output causes a deficit." He said, "Dogs would keep doing it over and over and over again, and sometimes it just depletes them of energy. Right now, we don't have any way to help as science hasn't caught up with energy medicine."

I was sick to my stomach. I had a tip on this directly from Samson himself, and I missed it. My friend Renata had also texted me on December 23 and 24 last year, asking about Samson. "The universe is telling me to check in on you boo boo. You doing okay?"

I had texted back, "Yes I think so LOL except Samson has something wrong with him that I can't figure out." She said, "Maybe keep a close eye on Samson. I had a dream about him, but I don't remember the details. I kept seeing your last name yesterday as we drove. Everywhere! And I finally thought, I need to reach out to Gale, and as soon as I thought it, I immediately saw another business sign with your last name on it."

I said, "Oh man. I hope he's okay. He's really limping today. He's definitely slowing down ☹️"

I'd also called Renata on the phone to ask more about the dream. She relayed she'd seen him in the dream in a place where she's usually visited by dogs who have passed.

Hindsight is always 20/20, but these interactions are just heartbreaking to me, as I now have so many other signs pointing to December as the time when his illness really started.

Back to reality. Matt and I boiled the chicken and rice and prepared all the vegetables he'd bought the day before. I made a pureed slop with some of the veggies and chicken broth, which was supposedly a surefire way to get the dogs to eat their veggies. I was gutted when Samson wouldn't eat any of it. Not even the boiled chicken, which was usually his favorite. Luckily, we also had some rotisserie chicken in the house, and he was happy to eat that. All the books and blogs on dog cancer say diet is the most important thing. Since he wouldn't eat healthy food for me, I ordered some functional mushrooms in tincture form that I could more easily get into his mouth. My research suggested we try Maitake, as well as a blend that included Turkey Tail, Reishi, and Lion's Mane, so I ordered those.

Saturday, May 4th

We decided to spend the day in the backyard and plant our garden. That morning, we drove Samson to a local nursery to buy some flowers, herbs, and vegetable plants. He enjoyed saying hello to some kids and other dogs. Always the socialite! There was a long line, so I sat on the cool concrete in the shade with Samson while Matt paid for our haul. All the customers who walked by couldn't help but smile at my baby boy. His zest for life was infectious.

My sister came by our house to see Samson that day. She and I sat with Samson on the back deck and in the dark green grass of our postage stamp of a backyard while Matt planted the raised bed garden. We soaked up much love and gave him many pets. I took videos to capture his good moments, which still seemed to happen quite often. However, Samson was starting to eat less and less, so my sister offered to order him some food from the pet store where she works. She said we should try canned food, and she selected a few options. She also researched treats that were full of fruits of veggies and relatively healthy. Unfortunately, we'd learn over the next few days that Samson was not interested in much of it. Another blow on the food side. Absolutely devastating.

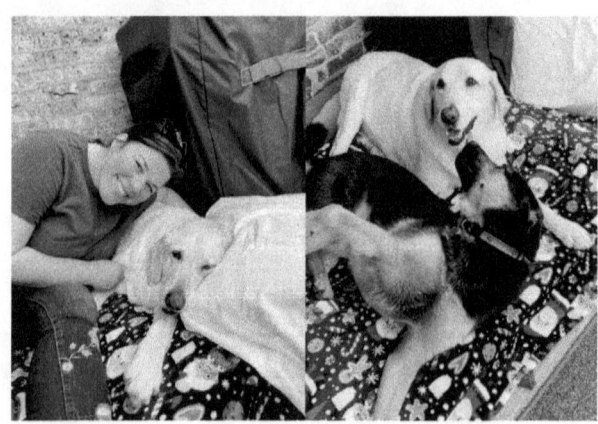

Aunt Laura's visit.

I did what I always do when stuck—I asked for help. I decided to put it out there and posted this on Twitter, now X, and LinkedIn:

> Anyone have resources or tips for dog cancer? Any insider info - stealth startups with miracle cures, new therapies to prolong life that aren't debilitating, anything you've tried that has helped with diet and liver function, etc.??
>
> I wish I was asking for a friend. My pup was diagnosed with liver sarcoma a few days ago. I've opted to do no operation or chemo/radiation as those aren't likely to work anyway. Keeping him comfortable, and he is still in great spirits and eating. Trying to find out how to get my hands on sorafenib if anyone knows. Sadly it looks like 1 out of 2 senior dogs meet this fate so I figured I'd ask! 🙏 🐶

I got a lot of great tips and advice. Functional mushrooms, curcumin (turmeric), broccoli, milk thistle, dandelion root, CBD oil, Apocaps, and Yunnan Baiyao were all supplements that could be helpful based on Samson's cancer. I ordered the few things I hadn't already come across and started giving him the milk thistle, turmeric, and CBD oil I already had on hand.

I had my second call with Mary Helen, the animal communicator, this afternoon. I told her Samson was diagnosed with cancer, and I wanted to know how he was feeling. She opened with, "Samson—he's sitting with it."

Then Murphy popped in. She said, "Murphy is a super sensitive dog and is very aware of your concerns about Samson. I sense tears and upset from him."

Mary Helen went on. "Samson has been the energizer bunny and keeps going and going, and we don't have a time for them to leave us in the forefront of our mind. It's always seemed as if he'd be with us forever. Samson is really a good boy, and he knows it. He has done a lot in his life. Through his perspective, he looks at it as an experience."

Mary Helen asked him about the cancer diagnosis. He said he knows it upsets us a lot. She said, "He is very matter of fact about it. He knows to a certain extent that his time is now winding down more quickly. It feels like there is something large for him. I don't know if it's a large tumor or large organ. Liver or whatever it is—feels like it's oversized. That is part of his issue. He is acknowledging that."

She shared, "He is not visiting the other side yet. Once he gets further down the road, he will get to a point where it will go fast. He says he will deal with that when it comes, and he will not worry about it. And he doesn't want you to worry about it."

Mary Helen asked Samson if he had an idea of what he'd like to do when his soul gets to go. She relayed, "He shows me a rocket. It would be like a blast off. There's a part of this that is so important for him as an individual and a being." I assumed this had to do with the fact that he was handicapped in this life and would be ready to leave his crippled body behind.

Samson shared with Mary Helen that he wants to be a therapeutic dog in his next chapter. He said when he comes back, we'll know it's him because of how our heart feels. We'll see his eyes and the way the tail wags, and there will be an attraction almost like a magnet. Mary Helen said it would happen maybe four to six months after he passes.

SAMSON'S STORY

I asked if there were things he needed to do or experience before he died. "He really likes to go in the car and get a treat—a pup cup. He loves the rides in the car even though he has trouble getting in and out. He says it's about doing things together. He is just happy to be with you on the patio. It's a real wind-down time. It's a lovely moment on earth. He says that seeing the sunsets—some of those are magical, and he doesn't mind that someday he will be part of a sunset for you."

Mary Helen didn't sense any apprehension from Samson about compartmentalizing things, and she said, "He's not going to worry about death until it gets here."

"He doesn't have any concerns about what you do or don't do. He said you can give him pain medicine, which will help." I asked if there was anything special he wanted to eat. Mary Helen shared, "You might offer him something really good like steak. The idea of new stuff is exciting to him—it's about the possibilities. Even if he gets to a point where he can't eat, the offering is important to him. He doesn't like the supplements at all—he turns his nose up at that. Giving him special treats like pup cups or ice cream—he loves it."

I asked Mary Helen how much time he had left. She said, "There's a part of the tumor that will behave itself, and part of it won't. He is just very realistic and matter of fact about it, and he's saying it's okay. He understands this organism called cancer will become like a flock of birds that swoop in and pick up all the seeds, eating everything off the ground. And all of a sudden, they fly off and move on to another area. It's more like that organism will be taking sustenance from him and feeding them. It's so odd he's showing me this. Whenever he leaves, he will go fast. He shows me it's like going in the car wash, and all of a sudden everything shuts off. You get your car washed and you go. One month feels a little premature—feels like he'll be here a little longer."

Sunday, May 5th

I had started sleeping on a mattress on the floor next to Samson's bed. When we woke up, I set up a camera on a tripod nearby and sang my good morning song to him. It was something I did most mornings—he loved when I sang to him even though my voice is not even good enough for an average karaoke song. "Good morning! Good morning! Mommy loves you! Mommy morning! You're your mommy's baby angel!" I knew the end was coming, and I didn't know how many more times I'd have to sing to my baby so I wanted to capture one on video that I could watch in the future.

I told Matt we should drive down to our old condo to see if Samson's friend Ziggy was still around. We hadn't seen him in years, but it seemed like the right thing to do. We didn't see Zig inside the fence where he used to live so we decided to park by our old condo and walk around. The downstairs neighbors' big fluffy doodle was outside in the building's gangway watching passersby, something that Samson loved to do on occasion when he had lived there three years ago. We gingerly pulled Samson out of the back seat and let him say hi to the neighbor dog while Murphy supervised from a few feet away. The young couple who lives in the first-floor unit where the two little kids who loved Samson had once lived came out when they heard their dog greeting Samson. I told them hello and explained that we were giving Samson a last stroll in his old neighborhood. They were sorry to hear about the cancer. Everyone was sorry to hear about it. What else could they say?

We walked around the block—a walk that was so familiar and yet so haunting to take, knowing the purpose of it and letting Samson get just one more look at a former chapter in his sweet life which was closing in on him swiftly. We got back to the car and drove a few short blocks east to where Samson's life with me had begun, at my first condo. As we drove over, I said to Matt, "I wonder if Charlie still lives here." Charlie was a yellow lab that lived one block north of us, and we had seen him in the park nearly every day for the ten months Samson was there back in 2017 and 2018. We turned a corner, very close to our destination, and lo and behold, I saw an older yellow lab walking with a man I recognized. "Matt, I can't believe it! It's Charlie and Brett! Pull over!"

Matt stopped the car, and I yelled out the window, "Hi Charlie!" I was sitting in the backseat with Samson, and I could see the confusion on Brett's face. Very understandable as it had been at least five years since I'd seen them! "I can't believe we ran into you! We were just talking about Charlie!" Brett replied, "It's so weird that we are out right now as we usually would have walked hours ago, but today was an off morning. And we just closed on a house in the suburbs and are moving out next week." How crazy. And magical. I knew it was no accident that we ran into Charlie. We lifted Samson out of the backseat and let him say hello to his old friend. We told Brett why we were there, and he said Charlie was now twelve and as all senior dog parents know, it can be right around the corner for any of us. I took a video of Samson and Charlie together, and amazingly, right by where we had pulled over, a husky was watching us from his window. Yes, you guessed it—it was Jameson, who must be seven years old now but was once the young husky puppy I had called Samson so many times that day in 2017.

Samson and his pal Charlie.

This was a moment where magic prevailed, and my tears were tears of joy rather than sorrow. But I had to keep going for Samson, as I knew things were going to get worse. I was very worried about his waning interest in eating, so I drove to a store in Chicago called Just Food for Pets and bought $100 worth of specialty food—venison, cod, and beef, riddled with lots of good and tasty veggies. I prayed he would eat it. My sweet boy sniffed it and turned his nose up at each one I had bought. Devastating. Luckily, Mrs. Grace, our neighbor, had a big bag of chicken jerky treats from Costco that he would eat. We thanked our lucky stars and gave him as many as he'd take down.

I made a short bucket list of all the things we wanted to do with Samson before he died—family pictures, dog park, dog beach, trip to Aunt Laura's, Home Depot, see his friend Stella at the park, and visit his friend Lucy in her backyard. I felt like a warrior—trying to learn as much as I could as quickly as I could while also loving him and letting him spend time in the places and with the people and dogs he loved most.

We were having a great day, so we decided to get started on the list immediately. We put Samson and Murphy in the car and went to the nearby park where we let them run off leash with their doggie friends. I took a blanket and a pillow so we could sit and hang out with the dogs longer than we usually do. We actually didn't use them because Samson and Murphy were pretty active the whole time. Samson met many dogs, his tail wagging the whole time. It felt like a pretty normal outing to the park except when we saw some of the dog parents we know and started to tell them about his diagnosis. It was really hard to say it out loud, but we knew it was an important step for us to start accepting what was coming.

Samson and Murphy in the park near our house, three days post diagnosis.

I also emailed our photographer to see if he could do some farewell pictures of Samson. Luckily, he was able to come the next morning, just four days after the diagnosis. I had gifted my sister and friend Peggy a photo session with their senior dogs, and I knew I should do my own final photo session while I still could. It was his sunset season, but I knew that if I could get some pictures as early as possible in this season, I would be happy I did.

We finished a very long and very good day with some cuddle time. I always relished having Samson up on the couch next to me. In the adoption and condo seasons, he loved to jump up by us quite often. In the seasons since then, Matt and I picked him up when he seemed to be asking to join us on the couch. On this evening, I took a picture of him snuggled up next to my legs on the chaise part of the couch. I knew how much I'd miss being able to cuddle my sweet, sweet boy like this, and my throat was one big lump as I savored the moment.

Samson next to me on the couch after our long day.

Monday, May 6th

I am so thankful that Albert, our photographer, who we'd worked with once per year since our wedding back in 2019, was able to meet us on Monday morning, just four days after Samson's diagnosis. It's a strange thing to want to take professional pictures at the end of your dog's life. This is not really how we want to remember them, but it's also the last chance we have. I cried that morning as I got ready. What do I wear for the last time I'll be able to take photos with my boy? I decided on no makeup, a bright pink sweatshirt, jeans, and tennis shoes—just like I would wear on any normal day.

We met the photographer at 9:30 a.m. in the park we'd been in the afternoon before. Samson was a bit tired from so much fun the day prior, but we were able to meet a few dogs in the park and take some pictures. Samson saw a black doodle on our walk back to the car. We told the doodle's mom these were Samson's last pictures and that he had cancer. She let us know that her dog also had cancer, which wasn't quite as aggressive but scary nonetheless; it was the first of many times people opened up to us once we shared what we were going through.

Our last set of professional photos with Samson in the park near our house.

The photographer, Matt, Samson, and I drove back to our front yard, another place Samson loved, to take a few more photos. He was pretty tired after the short session, but he was perky enough to get what we hoped would be at least a few good shots with us.

Our last set of professional photos with Samson in front of our house.

I had already cleared my calendar at work as much as possible. I decided to put up an out of office:

> Thanks for your note. My senior pup was recently diagnosed with cancer, so I will likely be slow to respond. I am trying to spend lots of quality time with him—I really appreciate your patience!

It was impossible to know how much more time we had, so I had to lean into being present and soak up as much of the good as I could.

Samson used to take Matt and me on walks in years past. He'd walk as far away from home as we'd let him, and he'd always stubbornly pull us in the direction he wanted to go, which was always away from our house. He took me on a number of mini walks this day. He'd walk a bit and then lie down in a yard along our route. He gravitated towards busier streets, where he had a higher chance of seeing dogs and people that might stop to say hi. We met a young light brown Shepherd puppy named Lilly who was very exuberant and so sweet—Samson loved saying hi to her.

He also walked me across a bridge near our house after we said hi to Lilly. I took a video of Samson walking slowly in front of me. I sometimes hear words that seem to pop up out of nowhere from my spirit guides, higher self, or maybe even from other beings that are communicating with me. On this walk, I heard Samson say very clearly, "Mommy, the answer is always in nature," so I actually said this on the video right after it came to me. My boy was so wise. A master teacher. I've thought about this insight many times since he died.

SAMSON'S STORY

Samson walking across the bridge.

I let Samson keep walking to his heart's content. He made it pretty far considering his health. It took us an hour to walk the distance we would have walked in 20 minutes a year ago. When he was good and done, he laid down in a front yard, right by someone's house. I called Matt to come pick us up, and I sat on a nearby bench and watched my boy enjoy himself.

Back home, I was continuing my research, and I remembered something the Tennessee vet said that had stuck with me: "The high bile acids are what is most concerning in the test results." I'd had an animal healer tell me about alkaline water in the past, so I wanted to try it. Perhaps it could neutralize the acid in his body. We loaded the boys into the car that evening and went to the store. I bought two more rotisserie chickens because this was one of the only things Samson would eat, and I grabbed eight big bottles of alkaline water. I pushed the cart out, and I realized this was such a normal thing—Matt waiting in the car with the dogs while I ran into a grocery store quickly. On this trip, just like all the other trips, Samson sat in the backseat with his floppy golden ears pushed forward, watching and listening for me. Murphy was in the front seat doing the same thing with his pointy black and tan ears at attention. My heart caught in my throat as I realized I didn't have an unlimited supply of seeing this precious pair of boys anxiously waiting for me after a store run.

I swallowed my heart and put on a happy voice and took a video as I greeted my babies while I still could.

My two boys waiting for me in the grocery store parking lot.

Tuesday, May 7th

We were going to the cancer doctor on this day. I hated fasting Samson this morning, as he had not even wanted to eat the rotisserie chicken last night. I didn't want the oncology vet to do any tests. We just wanted to discuss some options, but they insisted we bring him in fasted for eight hours just in case. Our appointment was at 2 p.m. in the afternoon, so we woke Samson up at 3:30 in the morning to take a gabapentin and eat something. He didn't eat much, but at least he got his pain medicine with some peanut butter.

That morning, I sat by Samson on his dog bed and did some work. Even though I wasn't able to completely offload all my responsibilities, I enjoyed being able to sit right by my sweet boy and pet him when I wasn't typing.

That afternoon, Samson did his usual tour of the vet's office. It was a new vet, but he strolled through and said hello to everyone, sniffing all corners of the reception area, just like he'd done at all of his many vets over the years. He was always very popular in vets' offices, and today was no different.

We were taken to a room while the oncologist reviewed the tests from last week and gave Samson a physical exam. She then joined Matt and me in our small exam room, and said she agreed with the other two vets about his diagnosis of carcinoma with an estimated survival time of one to two months. We declined options including radiation, chemo, and surgery, as we didn't want to put him through difficult treatments. The oncologist said we could try a pill called Palladia, which is a chemo-like drug that sometimes kills cancer cells. It's in the same family as Sorafenib, which I had found in my research, but there was more clinical data for Palladia, so we agreed to try it. The oncologist said he might have six to eight months if the pill worked. She gave us a two-week supply of the medicine, and we headed home.

Since Samson was no longer eating rotisserie chicken, we hit a Burger King drive-thru on the way home and prayed he'd eat a beef patty. He ate a bit of it, but this day (five days post diagnosis) marked the true onset of his very spotty eating. He would eat sporadically from here on—sometimes a handful of chicken hearts, or beef livers, or the chicken jerky treats our neighbor Grace happened to have on hand. At this point, anything Samson would eat was fair game. We tried steak, dog ice cream, human ice cream, eggs, every type of dog treat under the sun, and a wide variety of fast-food burger patties. He turned his head away from most of it, but he did eat a bit of cooked beef, human ice cream, and the beef livers, chicken hearts, and chicken jerky. He was also taking an appetite stimulant drug, so we were heartbroken that he wasn't eating more.

By this time, he was also fighting me big time on taking his medicine and supplements each morning and night. This was very distressing to me. Samson had taken four to five pills twice a day for many years with no problem. He always loved coming in from his morning and evening walks and getting his peanut butter treat, with a side of hidden pills. He was still very strong except for his back end, so he'd now clench his jaw super tight when it was pill time. He absolutely did not want to take any of it, but I forced it down his throat with special dog peanut butter. It was our new routine to have a clean-up time after Samson's pills. The blueberry dog peanut butter I'd ordered online was pretty runny and usually ended up dripping onto his fur because he moved his head so much, trying to avoid the pills. I used a damp rag to wipe him off. I used another damp rag to clean his anal gland area as it was still leaking. Samson was always such a clean dog (he used to observe a daily ritual that we dubbed "Grooming Hour," where he'd meticulously clean his paws and face), so I knew he'd be more comfortable if we cleaned him often.

The oncology vet had given us a worksheet called Quality of Life Scale that helped us rate how Samson was doing on the HHH-HHMM Scale developed by Dr. Alice Villalobos. HHHHHMM stands for hurt, hunger, hydration, hygiene, happiness, mobility, and more good days than bad. These seven dimensions are rated by a pet's parent and can help assess if a pet's quality of life has declined enough to consider euthanasia.

Thrive Pet Healthcare Specialist's version of the framework (see Appendix 6) suggests that ratings of 5 and higher (on a scale of 1 to 9) across the seven dimensions are acceptable. The vet told us we should calculate his baseline score that evening and then re-rate Samson across the seven dimensions every few days to track his progress. If he were to fall below a 5 on anything, we should seek help.

As of that night, Samson's ratings were a collection of 5s, 7s, and 9s. The two most concerning dimensions were Hurt and Hunger, as he was definitely in some pain, and it was clear he was not eating well by this point. We also scored him a 5 on mobility, but that was normal for us, and we knew how to manage it. We scored him a 7 on Hygiene, Happiness, and More Good Days than Bad. He only got a 9 (the top score) on Hydration.

Wednesday, May 8th

Samson's pills and supplements now consisted of levothyroxine (for his hypothyroidism), Gabapentin for pain, milk thistle, curcumin, cordyceps mushrooms, maitake mushrooms, reishi mushrooms, fish oil, CBD oil (an anti-nausea medicine and appetite stimulant), and the Palladia. We gave him his first Palladia pill this morning. I had to use latex gloves as the oncology vet recommended not touching the pill. As you can imagine, there are probably side effects from a pill you're not supposed to touch. We were to watch for vomiting, diarrhea, and any other adverse reactions. The oncologist suggested we reduce his dosage if we were to see any of that.

He had a pretty good day, though it started off in a bad way when I noticed a slight tremor in Samson's neck shortly after pill time. My heart dropped. It looked like he was shivering in his throat area, which was truly scary to see. I took a video and sent it to the vet in Tennessee to get her thoughts.

Not forty minutes later, I was taking a second video of Samson wagging and having a grand old time meeting a dog. It was a lot of up and down emotions at this point. The rest of the day was pretty good. He laid by the street again for a few hours, and I sat out there with him passing the time with lots of pets and a few games of Wingspan on the Nintendo Switch.

I didn't have a lot of work meetings at this point, but I did keep a scheduled Zoom meeting with one of our part-time team members who lives in Sweden. She asked me how I was doing, and I started crying. I told her how hard it was to watch my boy decline. She started crying as well and opened up about her dog that passed away last year. It was moments like this that made me realize how little we actually talk about the profound grief and sadness of pet loss.

Matt and I took Samson to the local dog park that evening. He had a ball and loved seeing and saying hi to other dogs. He even got some loving from a Bernese Mountain dog, just like normal. You see, Samson was always a popular boy for some reason, and although we had to pull the dog off immediately because Samson was so weak, it was a strange sense of normalcy to see this happen!

Samson having fun in the dog park.

We'd been openly telling everyone about Samson's cancer, and I was starting to kick around the idea of doing a Facebook post so all of his friends in the neighborhood would be able to come say goodbye to him in his final months. There was one special person that I felt compelled to alert. I didn't know this lady's name. Matt and I refer to her as "Hey Little Baby" because that is what she'd always say to Samson. She lives in our neighborhood, and we would sometimes see her walking her little dog named Cookies. Without fail, every time she saw Samson, she would run up to him and say "Hey little baby! Hey Mister!" She often kissed his head multiple times during these encounters, and it was clear that she loved him.

When we left the dog park that day, I told Matt we needed to find her. We knew the cross streets where she lived, and she just happened to be getting out of her car when we drove up. I was sitting in the back seat with Samson and got out when we saw her. I could tell from her face she was surprised to see us, probably since we'd been gone for so many months. I told her he was sick and let her sit by him in the backseat. She doesn't speak great English, and I don't speak great Spanish, but I think she understood that he didn't have a lot of time left. She told me that her mom's yellow Lab had also died of cancer. I think Samson brought her so much joy because seeing him reminded her of her mom's yellow Lab.

I fought back tears as she spent six or seven minutes in the back seat of our car with my boy. This lady really loved him, and I was so happy that she got to say a proper goodbye to him just in case we didn't run into her again.

We made it to the end of his first day of taking the Palladia, and we hadn't noticed any nausea, vomiting, or unease. He had continued to poop normally, so that was good too. We were hopeful!

Thursday, May 9th

I took Samson with me to drop off Murphy at day care, and then we went on a short drive to get a coffee and donut at a coffee shop called Caravanserai. I hit one of those white poles separating the bike lane from the parking spot with Samson's car, but I didn't care. My boy was still alive, and he sat in the backseat while I ran in, just like always. We got home, and he ate a Milk-Bone in the yard while I texted my friend Tyler, who I hadn't seen in a few years but had heard that his eight-year-old pup, Doak, was just diagnosed with bladder cancer. I told him about Samson's diagnosis, and he responded that he and Doak would love to meet up in a nearby park over the weekend.

I had a call with my executive coach that afternoon. Samson lay on the floor near my desk, and I sat by him on the floor just before my call. I had worked with this coach for nearly a year at this point, with calls every other week. This was the first time I'd talked with her since Samson's diagnosis, and she knew something was terribly wrong when I couldn't stop crying at the beginning of the call. I told her he had cancer and gave her a quick update on all that we knew. We were one week into the one- to two-month prognosis, and we were trying the Palladia.

Our call focused on what I could do to honor Samson's life and legacy and also to care for myself in a difficult time. In summary, the themes I left that call with were:

- Learning to trust that I was doing everything right
- Being in the here and now versus thinking about the future
- Accepting that uncertainty is a place of possibility that can lead to new chapters

SAMSON'S STORY

Aunt Bailey came to see Samson that afternoon along with her pup Madeline. It was starting to become clear that dogs could smell something wrong with Samson, as most didn't want to stay near him. It was almost as if they showed respect by giving him space.

After Bailey and Madeline left, we took both of the boys on a trip to Home Depot to get some paint for our rental unit. I also bought a small green and pink plant to replace one that had died in our front yard landscaping. Samson relished these trips and loved to sniff everything he could, especially in the garden section. We ended the evening with a long walk in our neighborhood. We walked towards where Samson's yellow Lab friends Murphy and Flo lived to see if we might run into them. Though I didn't know it at the time, it would be Samson's last long walk. Matt picked us up near Murphy and Flo's houses even though we didn't end up seeing them. The good news was that we still weren't noticing any side effects from the pill, although he was a bit more tired today.

Samson's last trip to Home Depot.

That night I got some videos and pictures of me loving him. I also went upstairs by myself to write two cards on behalf of Samson. You see, Samson always wrote cards to people. I would put my pen to the card and the words would come forth. My writing always looked different when I wrote these cards, and Samson would sometimes write a few letters backwards or misspell words (i.e., "ewe" instead of "you"). I had a very late Christmas gift for Mr. Bobby, the garbage collector, and Samson was always the one who wrote his cards. And Daddy's fortieth birthday was coming up next month in June. I wanted to make sure Samson wrote the card while he was still alive, and boy did I cry when I wrote those two cards. In my heart, I knew he might not have a lot of time. I hoped and prayed the Palladia would work, but I knew there was a very good chance Samson wouldn't make it to Daddy's birthday.

Friday, May 10th

We gave Samson his second Palladia pill today and hoped for the best. Sadly, I noticed more neck tremors this morning. The Tennessee vet had suggested I massage Samson's muscles in and around his neck to see if I could ease the shaking. It did seem to help quite a bit.

After a bit of front yard time, I put him in the backseat of the car and took him with me to our old condo that we still rent out after failing to find a buyer during COVID. We met Uncle Randy, who would be doing some touch-up painting for the new tenants. Samson had gone to several of Uncle Randy's Fourth of July bashes in the past, so I wanted to make sure he got to see Samson. My boy was very tired this morning, so I let him lie in the car for an hour while I helped Randy get started on the painting, and then Samson and I headed home.

We made it just in time for the visit from Mr. Bobby with his garbage truck. Samson walked down his ramp to the yard and even out the back gate to see Mr. Bobby. Samson still enjoyed eating a handful of Milk-Bones, which was such a relief!!

SAMSON'S STORY

Getting Milk-Bones in the alley from Mr. Bobby.

I got a devasting text from my friend Tyler today. "I'm going to have to cancel our play date. I had to put Doak down today." I was gutted. Just six weeks prior, he'd been given a prognosis of six to nine months of life left. Doak made it about one and a half months, and we'd just set up our play date YESTERDAY. I felt numb as I tried to wrap my head around what happened to sweet Doakie.

At this point, I was still booked on a flight to Nashville for an event the following day. I was doing the calculus in my mind: they had given Samson one to two months, and we were just over one week into that time period. Could I fly in for the day and come back on the last flight? I really wanted to go to the event, and I had waited until literally the last minute to make this decision. In the end, I canceled the flight to stay with my boy, and I'm so glad I did.

Later that afternoon, Mrs. Tracy came by to clean the house for the first time since we'd returned from Nashville. She had become quite fond of Samson over the years, so I knew it was going to be hard for her. He was in the yard when she arrived, and I'd already alerted her about the cancer via text. She was so happy to see him and showered him with lots of love and a few tears too.

Samson saying hello to Mrs. Tracy.

I'd been doing a ton of laundry—many towels, rags, and blankets—to keep things clean for Samson. It was a very cruel punishment from the universe when our washing machine broke that afternoon. I immediately found someone who could come take a look, but the earliest appointment was three days away. This was not ideal, as we were then doing at least two and probably up to four loads of laundry a day.

We had lots of visitors in addition to Mr. Bob and Mrs. Tracy that day. Aunt Laura and Aunt Sarah came by during the day, and Samson also got to see our new neighbors, who happened to be old friends, including their beautiful bull mastiff Winnie. We were having a pretty good day, so we took Samson to the dog park again after we picked up Murphy from school. This time, Matt lifted Samson into one of the kiddie pools in the makeshift "splash pad" area of the dog park. He seemed to enjoy the quick dip in the pool. As always, Samson loved seeing dogs and walked around for about twenty minutes before we headed back home.

SAMSON'S STORY

Samson in the kiddie pool at the dog park.

Peggy and Paul came over that evening and had some drinks with us by the fire we built in a Solo Stove on the tiny patio in our backyard. Things kind of felt normal when they were with us by the fire, as they had been so many times before. Murphy and Samson laid on the back deck with us just like they always did on fire nights. It was moments like these that were really nice because you could forget about the cancer for just long enough to have your perfect life back.

But things can change on a dime. And this time it was Murphy, who is a very loving dog but also extremely serious about protecting our house and family. Although he loves Uncle Paul, he didn't like that Paul went into the house first, and he lunged at Paul. This was not good behavior. I tackled him to make sure I could control him, as we didn't need the stress of a dog bite on top of Samson's cancer. We believe Murphy may have been hypervigilant at that time in order to protect his sick brother. But it was not something we expected to have to deal with, so I made a mental note that we'd need to talk with a dog trainer ASAP.

Saturday, May 11th

I finally posted about Samson's cancer on Facebook. In the last few days, we had scared a few people who came across him sleeping near the street, so I figured I'd be transparent about why we were doing that, as well as invite people to come say hi.

> Hello! My sweet boy Samson has loved living in our neighborhood these past 3 yrs. He was sadly just diagnosed with liver cancer, and I've found that one of the things he likes more than anything is lying down on our walks and hoping to meet dogs for sniffs and people for pets. If you see us around the neighborhood, please stop and say hi. It will truly make his day. 🖤✨

The response to this post blew my mind. 310 likes and 81 comments, all from our small neighborhood group. I think people loved Samson because he had such a big spirit, and he loved everyone he met—dogs and people—so much. One of the dog dads we saw on our walks every few weeks commented, "Samson is the 'happy' mayor of the neighborhood. I always smile when I see his 'happy hop' when he sees a friend. Hope to see you soon." Another neighbor we'd never met before offered to throw him a party in the park, which we set up for Wednesday afternoon. And another person I didn't know said, "I am sorry I crossed the street this morning during my dog walk hoping to give Samson privacy . I will make sure to bring my little yorkie teacup over to say hello."

I also decided to do some energy work on Samson, which included a tarot card reading, crystals, lighting a candle, and a ritual from one of my books to ask the bad stuff to leave him and invite healing energy in. I poured every ounce of my being into this, as I would have literally done anything to help my boy. I asked my spirit guides and animal helpers to please keep the pain away and give him more quality time.

Trying some energy work on Samson.

We had a happy meeting with a dog named Ace for the first time today while sitting outside. Even though I'd never met Ace before, he lived with his family just one street over. Ace was a black and white miniature Bernedoodle who LOVED Samson and was very happy to see him. At this point, many dogs were giving Samson his space, but I know he preferred the hustle and bustle type hello with lots of wiggles and wags that Ace was giving him right now. My heart was happy for my sweet Samson.

We were still sleeping downstairs with Samson, sometimes on the floor with him and sometimes in our guest bedroom. This night, Samson gave Daddy's arm a lot of head nudges for pets. If you ever laid by Samson and he wasn't sleeping, it was very normal for him to use his paw or snout to ask for more love. It was times like this that made things feel very normal and happy. As we got ready for bed, I set my alarm for 3 a.m. just in case it was clear enough to see Aurora Borealis from our house in Chicago. No dice on seeing Aurora's pinks and greens, but in hindsight, it was quite fitting to have a once in a lifetime sky show triggered by a geomagnetic storm during Samson's sunset.

Sunday, May 12th

We left early in the morning for Montrose Dog Beach. It's a lovely spot for the dogs to play in the sand and water, and Samson and Murphy have always loved going there. As we crossed Lake Shore Drive and the marina popped into view on our right side, Murphy recognized where we were and started to whine with anticipation. Samson perked up a bit, probably in response to his brother's excitement. Several of the roads leading to the public beach were roped off. Unfortunately, there was a bike race in progress that prevented us from parking close to the beach where we typically do. Rather than leave, we decided to see if Samson could make the walk, and we knew we may have to carry him if it proved to be too much.

Luckily, he did fine on the walk through the grass to get to the beach area. It was a cool morning, which I know Samson loved. Rather than take the long route through the main entrance to the beach and past the bay of dog wash stations, we saw a shortcut by the large rocks that others were using. Matt picked him up and helped him down the big gray stone steps. Samson teetered a bit on the sand and followed his brother the short distance into the water. I rolled up my yoga pants and stood in the water with my boy and helped him stay stable while the soft waves lapped by him and onto the beach. It was a bucket list item for me to get him here at least one more time, as he loved this place. I could tell he was quite happy to be here today. While Murphy said hi to other dogs and retrieved the orange and blue Chuck-it ball we'd throw out into the water for him, Matt and I took turns sitting with Samson where the sand meets the water.

Montrose Beach was the last place I'd seen my dog-nephew Cooper three years ago, right before he passed away at the age of fourteen.

SAMSON'S STORY

I could tell on Cooper's last day at the beach that he couldn't get around very well, and as I sat in the sand with my feet touching my boys' paws, I knew he was in a very similar spot. But I pushed that to the back of my mind. I wanted to be present for Samson. I took pictures of him, I got a video of him shaking the lake water out of his beautiful yellow fur, and Matt and I let him dawdle and say hello to many more dogs before we picked him up and carried him over the stone steps to leave the beach.

Samson's last trip to Montrose Dog Beach in Chicago.

We helped him to the car, and I sat in the back with him, windows down of course, on the way home. We gave both dogs a bath in the alley behind our house right after we got home. I knew it might be Samson's last bath, and I cherished it. My son loved to be clean, and I wanted to make sure he was as comfortable as possible. We then enjoyed lots of front yard time and saying hello to neighbors as they passed by.

I had made an appointment to talk with Jaime Breeze, the other animal communicator, that afternoon.

She connected with Samson and started the session. "Samson comes through so humbled and has a happy demeanor about him.

He's a very old soul, genuine, caring, kind. He's still appreciating life. Being outside is extremely important to him right now. It's empowering for him. He loves his day-to-day routine. He's not needing or expecting much. He's happy to relax and just be. He's not bored."

Just like he shared with Mary Helen, he said he has no fear about what was happening to him. Jaime relayed, "He puts his right paw on you—he says that is his way of saying 'there there' and comforting you. He's trying to tell you it's okay."

In addition to his hip issues, Samson told Jaime his knees, elbows, and top two canines were painful. Jaime asked him what his plan was right now. "He says he wants to enjoy the summer weather and eat a lot of meat off the barbeque. He's showing me he's thirsty. And then going to the liver, he shows me milk thistle." I told Jaime he wasn't a fan of the milk thistle pills I gave him. She said, "Try again with the milk thistle—maybe a tincture. He's also showing me iron." I told Jaime that he had been diagnosed with anemia as well.

I asked Jaime if the Palladia pills were okay. She didn't get a strong yes or no on the Palladia.

She asked, "Is there a solo armchair he sits in?" I said no, but he was with two other families before I adopted him in 2017, so it could be from one of them.

"He shows me that he just wants to have fun this summer as long as he's not feeling sick, so keep using the anti-nausea pills. Give him the best summer of his life. He did show me ice cream—vanilla. He shows me this older man who's on the other side." I told Jaime I believe his first dad had passed away and that is why he was initially given up for adoption.

She continued, "This older man whistled or had a whistle, and I feel the armchair Samson showed me earlier was connected to this man. Samson shows me it's a real comfort that this man is there to guide and help him. Samson shows me you writing letters or in a journal to him, and he really wants you to do that." She asked, "Have you ever considered or thought about writing a book? Samson shows me he helps you write this book before he reincarnates back. He opens the book for me, and there's a paw print of him in the pages."

Samson told Jaime we need to get the book written before he comes back. He said he wants to come back as a similar puppy—golden in color—some kind of lab or retriever. When he showed Jaime putting his paw on me in his current life, it's his right paw. In the future puppy body, he uses his left paw. She relayed, "Regarding finding him again, he says he'll tell you when to look and how to look and where. You'll see a picture of the new dog on a computer at some point."

"Samson wants to come back in a better body, and he wants to be a spokesperson. He wants to be in front of everyone. He wants to be a public dog, and he shows me a lineup of people he is helping in this new life."

I mentioned we plan to foster a dog before we adopt a new puppy. "The foster will work for you. I feel like you'll foster a pretty female lab. Murphy will get along with her quite well."

Jaime ended the session by offering to check in with Samson anytime. She said that right now, he seemed so happy.

Monday, May 13th

This morning, I realized I had only given Samson one Palladia pill on Wednesday and one on Friday, but he was supposed to be dosed two pills each time. So today I gave him two pills and hoped that the increased dose might help him get better faster. I knew it also might make things worse. Such a terrible decision to have to make.

We spent more time in the front yard this morning, as I had canceled an event I was supposed to volunteer at today. Nothing else was more important than being with my boy, and I felt so much gratitude that I was able to work from home and minimize meetings. It was today that Samson started to prefer Uncle Danny's yard across the road for some reason.

That afternoon, Matt and I took Samson for acupuncture, as this was the first available appointment the vet had when I called to book right after his cancer diagnosis. The vet and vet tech commented on Samson being their best-behaved and calmest acupuncture patient of all time. He couldn't stand for long periods of time, so he laid on a big comfortable mat while they worked on him. Samson seemed very tired, but he enjoyed the many pets he got from the vet tech while the doctor was putting in the needles. Twenty-four needles in total.

On the way home, we stopped at Burger King and got him an ice cream cone. Matt sat in the back seat with him, and I got a video of my happy camper licking up his vanilla ice cream.

SAMSON'S STORY

Samson loved ice cream cones during his sunset!

That night, Matt and I were a bit concerned, as Samson hadn't pooped since Friday (three days prior). I emailed the vet in Tennessee, who suggested we try an enema, so we planned on calling our Chicago vet in the morning. We also realized with regret that we hadn't been giving Samson the right amount of appetite stimulant. We gave him only one-tenth the amount prescribed, as I was surprised that the vet would have only given him a three-days' supply and not thirty. It was in a vial in metric units, which explains how we messed up by a factor of ten. We were giving him 1/3 of one syringe instead of three full syringes. Doh. We corrected the dose that evening and tried not to beat ourselves up about the mistake.

As I was cleaning up from the day, I walked outside to check on Samson. He was moseying over to the end of the deck, just like he often did to say hello to his favorite neighbor, Mrs. Grace, across the fence. I started walking faster, as he seemed a bit wobbly and was getting close to the stairs. I got there just in time to see him tumble down all six stairs. I screamed for Matt and ran to him. I can't believe I let my boy fall down the stairs. He seemed to be okay, and we quickly barricaded the top of the stairs with the outdoor lawn furniture to make sure Samson would stay safely on the deck when he was outside. What a way to pour salt on a wound when I already felt like we had failed him time and time again.

Tuesday, May 14th

Samson was very tired and didn't eat much, despite a correct dose of appetite stimulant that morning. I made a vet appointment for their first available time, which was at 6 p.m. Samson was so weak that Matt had to carry him from our car to the exam room.

We told the doctor our concern that he hadn't pooped in four days now. But that ended up not being our biggest worry. Samson had a fever of 104, which was quite high compared to his typical temperature of 102. The vet was concerned he may have pneumonia, so panic set in for me as I realized I may have to put my dog down on the spot if he were battling both cancer and pneumonia. They suggested a chest X-ray to see about the pneumonia. We agreed. The vet also took an X-ray of his colon since they had the machine on anyway.

Good news. The chest was completely clear, and not just of pneumonia but also of cancer. And aggressive cancers often spread to the lungs right before death, so this gave me some peace of mind. The X-ray of the colon also looked okay with nothing backed up, and the vet suspected the lack of poop was just due to not eating much.

Samson laid on the floor while the vet tech administered fluids under his skin, and we could tell this made him feel much better. We brought him home, and Matt and I reminisced a lot about Samson that evening. We went through old pictures and videos, texting each other the best ones we came across, like the one of Samson sitting by Daddy on the tennis court in Lanesboro during our honeymoon. Or the video of him walking through the two-foot-high snow drifts in the Catskills. We also made the difficult decision today to stop giving Samson the Palladia medicine, as it was making him extremely lethargic on top of his hypothyroidism and anemia.

Late that evening, after we went to sleep, Samson got up, and Matt let him go outside. He walked down his ramp into the backyard and moseyed on over to the gate at the front gangway, hoping Matt would let him out. Matt obliged, and Samson continued his slow walk down the gangway and through our small front yard. He crossed the street and laid down in Uncle Danny's yard. It was pouring rain throughout Samson's slow journey to what had become his favorite yard for a rest, and Matt had to lift him up to get him back inside. This was fairly distressing, as dogs tend to want to go off by themselves when they are ready to pass away. And Samson normally wouldn't have wanted to lie outside in the rain, so we were quite worried.

Wednesday, May 15th

Samson pooped in the yard this morning! I never thought I'd be so excited by a bowel movement. I just wanted him to be comfortable, and I was relieved to see him back to his "old" self of the past few weeks. He was very active today, moving from the deck to the yard to his indoor dog bed. I took a video of him walking through the backyard to send to his Tennessee vet team, who was rooting for him.

I emailed the short video along with an update on Samson and the doctor replied, "Glad that Samson is feeling better now. Fluids are a wonderful thing. As we discussed before, Samson doesn't know he has cancer. He is only thinking about today and how he feels right now. Quality of life is more important than quantity if working toward quantity makes you live longer but be miserable the whole time. I hope he has some months of good days for him and you. Thanks for the video!"

Aunt Laura came that afternoon and brought June, her fifteen-year-old foxhound. Samson was lying in Uncle Danny's yard, and he managed a big tail wag for Aunt Laura when he saw her. I was glad June came to see him, as she'd known him for almost seven years now. I always thought Samson would outlive June because she was a few years older, but here we were. We just never know when their time will come and have to enjoy every second with them.

Aunt Michelle also stopped by because she happened to be in the neighborhood. We sat in the backyard with Samson for a few hours while Michelle regaled me with her latest world travels and her new pursuit of a pilot's license. Samson was glad to see her too, as he used to go on many long walks with Michelle and me when we lived in the West Town condo. Back then, Michelle and I would walk up and down each street, admiring the hundred-year-old brick houses and sharing our joys and sorrows as we caught up on life. Samson was always out in front of us on these walks and would hang with us for two hours or more, stopping only for breaks when it was especially hot.

Right after Michelle left, Samson got a visit from one of his favorite humans—two-year-old Hazel. Hazel is often in her stroller and out on walks with one of her parents and their two tiny pups. She was really taken with Samson, and today was no different. She jumped out of her stroller, joined him on the ground, gave him a big hug, and said "I love you Samson." Talk about a tearjerker!

That evening was Samson's Facebook party in the neighborhood park. Matt and I drove Samson the short distance to the little park at 5:30 p.m. We saw his greyhound friends, June and Marty, and their mom gave us her condolences on Samson's cancer diagnosis. A few other people we knew, and some we didn't, stopped by to say hello to Samson. Another little girl, maybe five years old, kept lying by Samson and telling him how much she loved him. It was so sweet yet so sad to watch as these little girls had no idea how sick my beloved boy was. Matt and I thanked everyone for coming to see him, helped get Samson into the car, and then headed to pick up Murphy from school.

A little girl loving on Samson during his party in the park.

Thursday, May 16th

Samson had another acupuncture appointment late this morning. We were still without a working washing machine, so I dropped Matt off at the vet's office and took all of our dirty blankets, rags, and dog towels to the laundromat. I couldn't have my son sleeping on dirty blankets, and I knew in the back of my mind we were getting close to the end.

As the day went on, Samson wasn't doing terribly bad, but he also wasn't doing great. We revisited the worksheet from May 7th. It was still hunger and pain that were troubling us the most, and he now scored less than 5 on those two dimensions, which wasn't good. We were concerned that he hadn't eaten anything at all today, and he was so tired and weak. We knew the end was near if he was done eating, so Matt and I started making phone calls for at home euthanasia. We did a Zoom call with a recommended euthanasia vet late that afternoon and locked in an appointment for first thing on Monday morning. I would have four more sleeps with my baby. It was impossible to wrap my head around, but I knew we were at the end of the road. The Palladia hadn't worked, and we were out of options.

That afternoon, Samson was lying in front of our house and got to say hi to his yellow Lab friends Flo and Murphy (whom we called Big Murphy when he was around our Little Murphy). We luckily got Samson to eat some chicken hearts as evening was setting in, but I still had a tough phone call to make. Mrs. Amy, who owns the Magic Dog Bus, had surprised us with tickets to the Live Like Roo Gala in Chicago that was scheduled for Saturday night, and she would be flying in from Nashville to go with us. Live Like Roo is a wonderful not-for-profit organization dedicated to helping families and their dogs who are battling canine cancer. I had to break the sad news to Amy—Samson was at the end of the road and would be too weak for the gala on Saturday night. I expected that she'd cancel her trip to Chicago, but she said she'd still love to come and see Samson at our house.

I also shared the sad news with my sister, who came right away to see him. We sat by him on his inside bed next to where his ashes are now. He was snoring gently, and my sister captured a video to make sure I had a clip of this sweet sound to keep forever. When he breathed in, his peach and gray lip skin pulled in just enough that it made a "puff" sound when he breathed out. I loved watching his snout puff out ever so slightly with each exhale. He didn't do this very often when sleeping, as the angles of his nose and body had to be just right. I'm grateful I got to see it one more time tonight.

Perhaps one of the hardest things I did this evening was refill my boy's pillbox for the final time. Since adopting him, Samson had taken levothyroxine for his hypothyroidism along with fish oil and Dasuquin for his joints. In the last few years, he had also taken Carprofen and Gabapentin for his arthritis and nerve pain. Add in some Apoquel for allergies and a few random prescriptions here and there, and at least 10,000 pills have been loaded into his weekly pillbox with fourteen brightly colored individual compartments, one for each morning and one for each evening of the week. And it wrecked me that I only had to partially fill his medicine this time—there would be no more need for his pillbox come Tuesday.

I slept on the floor next to my boy. Samson was getting up often during the night to go in and out. He'd get a few hours of sleep on one bed and then switch to another. I don't think I slept much, or if I did, not very well.

Friday, May 17th

Matt and I took the day off, and we kept Murphy home from school. We decided to spend the beginning of the day in the large city park near our house where we'd done Samson's farewell photos. This park really sold us on the neighborhood and is a big reason why we bought the house we did. We'd probably visited it an average of ten times a week over the past three years, and Samson loved it.

We took chairs and found a patch of shade near the sidewalk. We typically walked out to the middle of the big field where the dog owners let their dogs run around off leash, but we couldn't make it that far today. Samson laid in the grass and got to say hello to lots of his dog friends that he often saw in the middle of the park. Kaleesi, his favorite German shepherd, stopped by. We hadn't seen her since we got back from Tennessee, so it was good timing. Kaleesi's dad, Tony, is a big teddy bear of a guy. He loves all the dogs and was especially fond of Samson because Samson always had a pep in his step when he saw Kaleesi. Tony bent over and petted Samson for a minute or two. He stood up and wiped tears from behind his glasses. He told me he remembered Samson woo-wooing all the time, and he hated to see him so tired. This hit me like a ton of bricks. I hadn't realized how different Samson would seem now to the people who came in and out of his life because we had seen his steady decline from the front row.

I propped up my phone on my backpack and used the timer to get one last photo as a family in the park we all loved. After two tries and ensuring everyone was in the frame, we packed up to make it home for Mr. Bobby's final visit.

Our last family photo in the park.

SAMSON'S STORY

At 11:45 a.m., I took my last video of Samson waltzing down his ramp as he heard the "beep- beep-beep" of Bobby's truck. I went out the back gate and gave Bobby the bad news that this would be his last time to throw treats for my boy, as we'd made an appointment for Monday. He turned off the truck and came into our yard to say goodbye to Samson. He asked if we really had to do it, and on cue, Samson had a bad diarrhea spell in front of Bob. Yes, he was very sick at this point. We had hoped Samson would be around for Bob's retirement, which was just one month away, but sadly we couldn't quite get him there.

Mr. Bobby came into the backyard to say goodbye to our boy.

I spent most of the day sitting next to Samson and writing his story on my laptop. I remembered my sister telling me how she told her chocolate lab Cooper his adoption story the last night of his life as she was saying goodbye to him, and I wanted to do the same for Samson. I was inspired to recount his whole story, including all the special details, so I went back through emails and texts and pictures to make sure I didn't miss anything. Once he'd been given one to two months to live, I had known I would do this for him while he was still alive. The time had come to write his story. At one point this afternoon, we were in front of Uncle Danny's house, and a small orange and black butterfly kept landing on Samson's stomach and then on my head, and back and forth, again and again. It was so odd that Matt even took a picture while it was sitting on my head.

Working on Samson's story. The butterfly is on my pink hat!

Samson's dog sitter, Cella, came to say goodbye to him. We also asked Tracy, our house cleaner, to please come today even though she'd asked to skip. We wanted the house to be clean for his last days. She agreed to come, but it was very hard for her as she absolutely LOVED Samson.

That evening, I finished writing his story, which was eight pages long in the end. I sat by Samson's outside bed where he was lying and began reading his tale to him, trying not to cry too much. I'd only made it a few pages when he got up and moved down to the yard. He seemed pretty uncomfortable and distracted, so I decided I'd finish reading it to him later in the weekend.

As darkness set in, we made a fire in the backyard. I walked down the back steps to the yard to give Samson his nighttime CBD oil, and I realized his body was shaking. It was pretty cold outside, and I know that Samson was in the grass because that is where he felt best—grounded and cool, with fresh air. But I knew he was too frail for this temperature, and he was just lying there, accepting the tremors. With tears stinging my eyes, I called Matt over and told him we should probably move up his appointment to the next morning.

SAMSON'S STORY

I had thought I still had three sleeps with my boy, and in an instant, there was just one. I gave him his pain medicine and let him continue to the lie in the grass despite the shaking. I sat about fifteen feet from him by the fire and read him his whole story while tears streamed down my face. He wasn't right next to me, but I knew he could hear it, and I wanted him to know how special his life was and how special he was to us. Every last detail.

With just one sleep left, we decided to join Samson on the back deck for a night under the stars. We took our twin fold-up mattress and the two indoor dog beds out there, along with lots of blankets and pillows. Murphy, Matt, and I curled up next to Samson for his last sleep ever. What was I going to do without my sweet yellow boy???

Saturday, May 18th

We've cycled back to where this book begins, on the day he left us.

We woke up early with the sun at 5:30 a.m. I didn't mind though because it would be my last day with my boy, and I wanted all the time I could get. We made some phone calls early that morning and changed the euthanasia appointment from Monday to today at noon.

I texted Mrs. Amy, who was supposed to come visit us today: "Sorry for the early text but I want to get you before you leave for the day. Samson really went downhill last night, and I'm afraid he definitely won't make it until his Monday appt. We are going to say goodbye today. I am so grateful you were planning to come and see him, and I'm just heartbroken that he couldn't hang on long enough for a little more time with all of us. Just 3 weeks ago, we were having our last Sat in Nashville which was a great day, and I had no idea he was on this path. 🥺"

A few hours later, I Facetimed Amy so she could say goodbye to him. The morning was a blur, though I spent as much time with my boy as I could. Car rides and lying on the back deck were two of his favorite things, and I'm grateful we got to do both with him on his last day.

I'd been putting off communicating with him about what's to come. But we didn't have any time left, so I connected with Samson telepathically and asked him how he planned to send signs to us once he was gone. He told me he'd send yellow retrievers, birds in unusual places, and green and pink surprises. I did one last tarot reading for my boy, and it was quite fitting that he pulled two kings. The king card is a very strong and positive card in the tarot deck that conveys a wise man—an inspiration and motivation to others. One was the King of Roses, the suit of love and family. It was a perfect reading for my Samson—one of inspiration and love.

Some of our last moments with Samson, giving him as many pets as we could.

After we said goodbye to our sweet boy, which ended in the magic and wonder of the flock of birds synchronicity, Matt, Murphy, and I were left to begin the first day of our new normal. We wanted to get out of the house, so we took Murphy for a long walk right after the vet left with Samson's body. At first, I felt relief for Samson. He was no longer in pain and was flying free at last. The initial high was reinforced on the walk when we saw a duck waddling on the sidewalk right in front of us. I'd never seen a duck there, and I knew it was Samson sending me a "bird in an unusual place." I thanked him and prayed I would see more signs from him.

I had to keep myself busy, so I went with Matt to my office downtown and cleaned out the kitchen. The next day was our neighborhood garage sale, which would be a nice distraction, and the upcoming end of our office lease meant it was a good time to sell off some items.

That evening, our friend Peggy came over to hang out and spend the night in advance of the big yard sale—an annual event in which fifty or so neighborhood homes participate. We made a fire in the backyard and had some drinks in honor of Samson. My old friend Jerry used to say you always pour out some alcohol when a pet dies, so we said a few words and poured out some beer for Samson. Around 10 p.m., I got a text from Amy: "Are you going to bed soon? I may be in Chicago, and I do NOT want to intrude, but I really want to hug your neck and give Murphy a big kiss. I can head back to the hotel or to you guys in 15 minutes! I also want to tell you about Live Like Roo!"

At that moment, I realized that Amy had still come to Chicago for the gala. Of course she should come say hi, so I invited her over. Amy joined us by the fire and recounted the Live Like Roo gala, which consisted of about 150 people and a few dozen dogs at an outdoor event space in the West Town area of Chicago. She said she was surprised tonight, as with no advance warning, they asked her to go up in front of the attendees and tell them about Samson. You see, Samson was being honored at the Live Like Roo event. Part of Live Like Roo's mission is to help families pay for their dogs' medical bills, and this gala was an event to raise money and awareness. Amy had nominated Samson to be a Live Like Roo dog, and we didn't know it, but if he and I had been able to attend, he would have been honored in front of all those people. They were going to pay for his medicine and cover the expenses of any items on his bucket list. I was so touched. And so devastated that he didn't make it just a few more days, as I would have given anything to see him at that event, still alive. He would have loved to be there and see all of the people. It was my first real taste of the conflicting emotions that ride shotgun with grief—love and pride for him coupled with despair that he wasn't here to do something.

Samson on the big screen at the Live Like Roo event.

Amy showed me a picture of Samson on the big screen at the event. I wished with all of my heart that he'd been there. That we had been there. That I was anywhere with Samson other than here on this evening of his death, without my beloved boy at my side.

I heard Samson's voice in my ear that night at the fire. He said, "Mommy, it's okay that I wasn't there. I didn't need the bucket list because I already did my whole bucket list. I loved my life, and you gave me everything I could have wanted. It should go to the other dogs and their bucket lists." It was the first time I heard him so clearly. Any animal communicator will tell you that it's tough to talk to our own animals because we know them so well, and that familiarity really gets in the way of trusting our intuition. But now that Samson was gone, I could hear him plain as day. A bittersweet discovery that at least I could still connect with my boy in spirit.

Chapter 4

WHAT TO DO WHEN THE END IS NEAR

I hope Samson's story provided some helpful context on how the end unfolded, including what went well and not so well. I'm grateful his last two and a half weeks were filled with intention and love. He got to do a lot of his favorite things, see people he loved, and he was wagging and happy for much of it. This chapter transitions to focus not on Samson's story but on the how-tos that might be helpful for you during this unthinkable time when you know the end is coming soon.

It's a huge shock to the system when you've just realized your pet has mere months, weeks, or even days to live. 89 percent of the survey respondents learned of or confirmed the poor prognosis of their pet at a vet visit. Of these pet parents, 43 percent received an estimate of the amount of time their pet had left to live, whereas 57 percent did not. In further research, I would want to better understand if the pet parent had to ask for the estimate or if it was just offered. In my case, I specifically asked how much more time Samson had, so that may be something to consider requesting from your vet if you want to know.

Among the survey responses where a vet's estimate of remaining time was given, 50 percent of pets lived fewer days than estimated, 30 percent lived more days than estimated, and 20 percent lived the same number of days as expected. It appears that vets are more likely to overestimate time left when a pet is given two months or less. My advice is to assume you are likely to have fewer days left with your pet than the vet's estimate suggests. Just like sweet Doak, who only lived six weeks of an estimated six to nine months and my angel Samson, who only lived sixteen days into a one- to two-month projection, your baby may not have as much time as you think.

In hindsight, I can say with 100 percent clarity that the best thing to do is focus on now. You somehow have to maintain your strength for your pet and for yourself. The following advice is written in the order I would approach it, though feel free to focus just on what's relevant for your situation, in whatever order best resonates.

Start with a Good Cry and Embrace Anticipatory Grief

When you first learn that you're at the end of the road with your beloved pet, it is beyond awful. So take the time you need to cry. Perhaps it's when you read this book or as you share the news with close friends. Maybe it's something you make time for each night after your pet goes to bed. Just make sure the crying is contained to the time you want to let it in. I did a lot of crying the first evening, and then I made a conscious decision to be there for my boy and try to make the most of the final time we had left. It's hard to enjoy anything when we're in agony. And pets are always in the "here and now." They aren't thinking about the past or the future, just this exact moment. They want to spend as much quality time with you as they can. If it doesn't seem like you can stop the crying and sadness, try to find a way, for your pet's sake.

SAMSON'S STORY

I am now in the process of preparing to deal with the death of my senior pet, Bacon, and the long runway of decline. I'm often curious what the process will look like this time since we can both see it coming, and not see it coming at all. Bacon is also somehow in great condition (will still bound up three flights of stairs after a walk!) and declining condition (is losing the ability to understand when his body needs to go to the bathroom), which is also expensive. Without sounding insensitive, there is a part to this decline where I can feel this isn't something I could manage forever. I am very curious how it will feel when we finally lose him, because it's harder this time around to feel like the time is limited and should be cherished, when so much of the time is spent truly caregiving and revolving around him. There is a shared path of frustration over how much our time and energy revolves around him, while also realizing I don't know what my life is without him (I was 26 when I got him, now 40) and won't have him to come home to, snuggle with, and take on adventures.

—Survey respondent

You've probably already realized the grief of losing your pet starts well before they actually leave this world. Anticipatory grief is just what it sounds like—you know what's coming, and you start to grieve the loss before they're gone. In addition to your good cry, you can lean on loved ones, therapy, Facebook support groups, and resources from grief experts to help process what you're going through.

Decide on a Treatment (or Non-Treatment) Plan

If your pet is sick and there's a chance you could help them get better or increase their quality time left, you could consider treatment options. Are there medicines, surgeries, therapies, supplements, or a special diet that might slow things down, reduce pain, and improve quality of life? Does it make sense to get a second opinion? Sometimes, an aggressive treatment plan is warranted. And sometimes, trying one or two things or even doing nothing is the best path forward.

While we didn't opt for aggressive surgery or chemotherapy with Samson, we did try a few things. I don't regret taking him for a second opinion at the oncology vet or using the Palladia pills. But if I were to go through it again and could fully acknowledge how little he was eating and what that truly meant, I would skip the second opinion and spend that day with my sweet boy out on the lawn where he was happiest. I also don't regret trying to make and buy healthy food and snacks for Samson because I can rest assured that I did everything possible to see what he'd eat. I still have some PTSD from trying to feed him supplements in the last week or so, and I wish I wouldn't have forced those on him. The things I'm very glad we did for him are the acupuncture visits and administering fluids when he had a fever.

I'd aim to identify the right treatment plan, including any surgeries, medicines, supplements, special food, or vet visits you plan to try within one week of your pet's diagnosis, if possible. Call second-opinion vets immediately, because there could be a wait to get in, particularly if it's a specialty vet. Read any books and online resources you're drawn to, and talk with a trusted vet or two to make sure you feel 100 percent comfortable with your pet's treatment plan. It will be a lot to process, but pushing through it quickly allows you to check off the data gathering, learning, and major decision making so you can then focus on spending quality time with your pet.

Above all else, trust yourself to make the right decisions—you know your pet better than anyone else, including your vet, experts, and friends. Follow your gut on whatever it is you decide to do (and not do) for your pet and their treatment (or non-treatment) plan.

Add Safety Measures as Needed

The biggest thing I regret is not barricading the top of our back deck stairs. After reading a lot on the topic of end of life as I conducted research for this book, ailing dogs falling down stairs is not uncommon. I hate that Samson fell down our stairs during the last week of his life, and I want to prevent that from happening to your pet! Think through anything that might be unsafe for your pet and take measures to remedy it. You might move your rugs around so that they have better grip in high traffic areas or by their water bowl, add a full body harness to help pick them up when they need to go outside, or declutter their area to make things easier and less stressful for them.

Practice Mindfulness with Your Dog

I am not a big meditator. My mindfulness activities have always centered around dogs, whether it's a long walk with my dogs in the park or quiet time while petting a pup. The best advice I got from *The Dog Cancer Survival Guide* was to spend time with your pet each day and tell them what you're grateful for. I did this a lot with Samson in his last two and a half weeks—I'd sit next to him, pet him, and tell him out loud how much he meant to me and why I was grateful to be his mommy. Honestly, I wish I'd done this practice often throughout all of his golden years, and it will be something I do with future dogs as they age.

Make a Final Bucket List

You now know how you want to approach vet visits, medicines, and treatment plans, so let's transition to quality-of-life activities. What do you want to do with your dog in their final days and nights on earth? Get out some paper and write it all down. When you look back, after your dog is gone, what will make you smile? The activities could be big or small, and maybe you've done them a thousand times, or maybe they are once in a lifetime experiences. Maybe you take a trip somewhere special. Maybe you spend all your time in the backyard. Maybe you go get a pup cup from a local coffee shop or a vanilla ice cream cone from Dairy Queen. It's really up to you what would make the experience the best for you and your dog.

My list for Samson included seeing specific friends and their dogs that were meaningful to him, going to the dog beach, visiting the dog park, and going on lots of car rides. We didn't make it through every single item, but we did quite a bit of it. Having this list helped me focus on the things I knew Samson loved. If he was feeling up to it on a certain day, we made sure to do at least one item on his list. We had to cancel a few because he wasn't feeling well, but I am glad they were all planned because I know I did everything I could to give him the kind of send-off he deserved.

Acknowledge That Things Won't Be Perfect

Unfortunately, you can't architect your pet's last moments to be perfect. This will be an exercise in going with the flow. I dealt with a broken washing machine in Samson's last week of life, which was less than ideal with a sick pup. Typically, I would have lost my shit on Maytag because the washing machine had been such a dud even before it quit altogether at just three years old, but I put all that all aside for Samson. Just like when we took him to the dog beach and there happened to be a bike race. That was unlucky because I couldn't get him close to the beach entrance in our car. So, we had to improvise. Samson's last few weeks required a lot of patience and trust that even if things weren't perfect, I could still focus on the good things and not spin out about that which I couldn't control.

Find Joy in and Capture the Little Moments

I took a lot of pictures and videos of Samson during his final two and a half weeks. And I wish I had taken many more. In hindsight, there was so much joy he had when he got to greet people and dogs and go on mini adventures in the car. As I went back through my photo library to write this book, there were sometimes twenty-four to thirty-six hours that would go by without any photos of him, which makes me sad.

I give you all permission—take the photos and videos! You can always delete what you don't want later. Yes, it's important to be present and not waste time getting the perfect shot, but any little joyous moment you see might be a great opportunity to capture a memory. And I can tell you these photos and videos may be very healing for you once you're on the other side. I've gone back to them many times during my immediate grieving process, sometimes because I'm trying to remember what happened and sometimes because I want to see him smiling and happy in his last days.

Share the Experience with Others

There are friends, family, neighbors, and people at the dog park who are fond of your pet. You may wish to share the news sooner than later if that feels right to you. I'm very glad I put up an out of office with the news, posted on social media, and was open with people we talked to. I wanted everyone to know Samson didn't have a lot of time left, and anyone who loved him should come and see him. I knew it's what Samson wanted.

If this doesn't feel right to you for any reason other than societal pressure, that is totally okay. But if you just feel like you're supposed to keep this to yourself because society at large makes us feel lesser than for grieving a pet's death, I'd encourage you to consider sharing anyway. I was very touched by the responses I got when I was up front about what we were facing. Friends and strangers alike told me stories about pets they'd lost, tearing up sometimes years after they'd passed. A dozen people came to a party for Samson in our local park that a stranger in our neighborhood Facebook group hosted. I got countless offers of help when I sought recommendations at the onset of his diagnosis. Every single person who responded was very supportive.

And maybe most importantly, I think this step made things a lot easier for me to process. I put it out in the open, and once I did, I could really focus more on Samson rather than on my own feelings.

Readjust Your Time If Possible and Ask for Help

Can you take time off from work? Can you work fewer hours if someone covers for you? Are there things you can get off your plate right now (cooking, cleaning, laundry, childcare) that will give you more quality hours with your pet? While this may not be something everyone can do, it's worth critically thinking about and making adjustments, if at all possible.

I'm very grateful I was able to minimize work meetings during this time as well as pay a house cleaner to ensure everything was clean and orderly in Samson's last few weeks. My sister and neighbors were also willing to help with watching our other dog or bringing us food as needed.

If you feel overwhelmed or trapped in a routine that isn't giving you the time you need, please ask for help. Even if you think there's no way things could be better, please go to at least two people in your inner circle with a specific ask. You may be surprised by what a boss, coworker, friend, or family member is willing to do to make things easier for you right now. I'm confident there are at least a few (if not many) people in your corner who would want to do something to help. After writing this book and talking with many people about pet loss, I believe nearly all pet owners can empathize with how hard it is keeping your life together when caring for a dying pet.

While on the topic of receiving help from others, I want to touch on the topic of bereavement gifts. I personally wish that instead of sending flowers after a pet passes, we could make it mainstream to gift a cleaning session or a takeout meal. These gifts would be welcomed both before and after a pet passes. These things give us back an hour of time to spend with our pet if they are still alive, and we get the added bonus of not having to watch funeral flowers slowly die while we're already enveloped in death.

Make an End-of-Life Plan

If you have the luxury of some time before your pet passes, it's best to plan the end-of-life logistics in advance. If you're near crisis mode and your pet doesn't have much time left, this step is even more important to do right now.

The first question is to euthanize or not? Some people feel guilty about taking the life of their beloved pet. Others feel it's a humane and just decision if it prevents suffering and pain. Wherever you land on this decision, your pet will understand. I personally believe that if we can help animals cross over and avoid unnecessary pain, euthanasia can be viewed as a gift and the final caretaking responsibility we embrace with love and reverence.

If you decide euthanasia is the right path, you can opt for an in-vet or at-home appointment. A euthanasia appointment at your regular vet can be a low-stress option if your pet knows the staff and generally feels comfortable in that setting. Costs range from $100 to $300. An after-hours vet, such as an emergency vet, will be a bit more expensive, typically $200 to $400, and pet parents might opt for this option when their regular vet is not available. Another option is at-home euthanasia, and while it is a bit more pricey at $300 to $1,000, it may be the most calm and comfortable for you and your pet.

> I didn't feel guilt about Piper and Rookie's deaths, but a big part of that is because our vets told us our choice was humane. Neither vet pushed us toward a decision, but gently telling us that choosing to say goodbye to stop my girls' suffering was humane and an ok choice was immensely helpful.
>
> —*Survey respondent*

> I knew it was coming for a long time, but it didn't make it any easier. I always wondered what would be worse, knowing exactly when it was going to happen (by planning it) or it just organically happening. I think both are equally difficult.
>
> —*Survey respondent*

SAMSON'S STORY

I like how Samson's at-home euthanasia vet described pets as having a window during which euthanasia makes sense. While we would all like the appointment to be at the very last second of the window, it's more important that we say goodbye somewhere in that window rather than wait too long. My husband and I had collected numbers of three highly recommended at-home euthanasia services, and we kept those in our back pocket until we knew for sure that we were inside the window. We called to make the appointment once we knew we needed to say goodbye within a few days. It's possible that same-day or next-day at-home appointments may not be available, but we found that having a few recommendations at the ready made it pretty easy to secure a time that worked for our situation.

If you decide to go the in-vet route, take a used blanket or worn shirt with your scent on it. Keep this blanket or shirt close to your pet throughout the process as an extra comforting mechanism. You might even opt for an experience in another location like this:

> The process of having to put my dog Mishka to sleep ended up actually being very beautiful and helped with the grieving process. I was able to find a vet who could facilitate her sleep by the roses in the local botanic gardens - it's a whole story, but it was as beautiful a day as it could have been for her and I, as was the support of everyone I knew - friends and work alike.
> —*Survey respondent*

Regardless of which approach you take—no euthanasia, in-vet, at-home, or at-another-location euthanasia, the next decision to make is what to do with the body. Cremation and at-home burial are two common options. If you cremate, you can do a community version where your pet is cremated alongside a few other pets, and you will receive a portion of the ashes, some of which are your pet's. Private cremations are slightly more expensive, and just like the name implies, it will be only your pet in the crematory chamber and only your pet's ashes that you receive. If you cremate, make sure to request a paw print, nose print, and/or fur clipping if any of those are of interest to you. When we filled out the online form and selected private cremation for Samson, the form would only allow us to select one, so we chose the paw print. When the euthanasia vet came to our house, she said we could opt for all three, which I'm very glad we did. Having a 3" x 3" clipping of fur is something I cherish very much, so if it's not an option for you, consider taking your own clipping of fur before the euthanasia vet takes your pet's body away.

If you prefer to bury your dog, I'd at least consider what you would do if you end up moving at some point. Will you bid a final farewell or dig up your buried pet and take it with you? The positives of burial are that you can visit them in your yard at any time, and you can bury their favorite treasures with them. Please make sure you bury them deep enough so that other animals don't dig them up, and steer clear of any electrical, water, or gas lines. Check with your municipality first. A neighbor of ours found this out the hard way when they hit a gas line, and dozens of firefighters were on site during a somber time.

If you're still torn between cremation and burial, let me share a comment from one of our survey respondents:

> "We buried Bo, and it was at that time we both broke down. We decided if we had to go through this again, we would consider cremation due to our experience."

Take some time to consider who you want involved in your last day with your pup. Is it just you? Just you and your partner? Any other friends or loved ones? What will you do with any other pets in your household who might benefit from sniffing the departed pet for their own closure? For Samson, it was Matt and me with him in his final hour, but my sister did come by earlier to say goodbye. I also FaceTimed two friends to say goodbye to him, and in hindsight, I wish I'd called a few more to let them say goodbye. We also had a plan in place beforehand for our other dog. We dropped Murphy off at our neighbor's house fifteen minutes before Samson's euthanasia appointment, as we knew it would not be a calm environment if Murphy was present. While some pet siblings might do just fine to stay in the room, if yours is like Murphy, make sure you have a good friend or neighbor available to help you with the day's logistics.

Consider Some Extras If You Have Time

While your pet is still alive, you might want to organize their photos and videos, go through their belongings, and/or write them a story or poem. I was very worried I wouldn't be able to cope with some of these things after Samson died, but I didn't have time to do much except for write his story that I read to him the last night of his life. That felt like a fitting tribute, as I wanted to do some kind of memorial service for him while he was still with me.

I also encourage you to schedule a photo shoot of you and your pet if that speaks to you. If you want to do this, I suggest getting that calendared as soon as possible to maximize the chances your pet feels up to it. The Tilly Project is a resource you can use to find photographers who specialize in farewell photo sessions for pets.

Survive the Actual Transition (Death)

Beyond the logistical plans for the end-of-life transition, the actual death part is not something I was prepared for. I believe all dogs go to heaven, and I love the idea of the rainbow bridge. Dogs are such pure beings and full of love that the rainbow bridge has to be real!

As an animal communicator, I've talked with a number of dogs towards the end of their life. Their message is always the same when I relay questions from their parents, who are trying to understand if they should euthanize now or wait longer. Dogs tell me they trust their parents 100 percent. They say their parents will know in their gut when it's time to make the decision. If they make it now or wait longer, the dog is okay with either one.

I once spoke to a dog whose mom had already made a euthanasia appointment for the next day, but I didn't know that prior to my conversation. In fact, I didn't even know this dog, Harlow, was sick beforehand, but I always do a body scan to understand any issues the animal has. In this case, I could tell Harlow was slowing down and quite stiff in her joints and also had some pain in her left shoulder. Sometimes I sense or feel a very high level of pain with an animal, but I did not in this case. When I debriefed with Harlow's mom later in the day, I learned that Harlow had a tumor on her face that had grown quite large. Harlow's mom was very concerned about her and thought she was in a lot of pain. Harlow's reading echoes what I've experienced in many other readings—animals focus on the good and ignore their pain until it's unbearable. They want to stay with us as long as possible, as they find a way to lean into the good while they still can. Was Harlow's mom right to make a euthanasia appointment even though Harlow's body scan didn't indicate she was in crippling pain? Absolutely. Would she have been right to wait a bit longer? Absolutely. The good news is that pets are ready for their transition and do not fear it. They're happy to stay with us as long as it makes sense, but, once again, they trust us as their parents to make the right decision for them. So don't fret about the exact right timing. Just make sure you're in the window where it makes sense, and trust your gut just like your pet trusts you.

I was glad my house was clean for Samson's final day, and I'm so grateful I had clean blankets, especially after the washing machine debacle. I'm grateful my husband and I were with him at the end, telling him how much we loved him. I'm glad I had read in a book that a dog mom regretted that she sat by her dog's backend while her husband sat by the dog's face. I made sure both Matt and I were close to Samson's head while we said goodbye.

You might tell your pet their adoption story, like my sister did with her sweet Cooper as he passed. You might tell them how grateful you are to them or what your favorite memory was. You might sing a song to them, just like I sang Samson the final rendition of his goodnight song. Whatever you decide to do, be as present as possible, and be right there for your beloved pet. It's okay to cry and be sad, but try to send strength and love to your pet, as they can definitely feel all the emotions.

One of the regrets I've heard from a few people is that they didn't stay with their dog or cat while the vet administered the euthanasia drugs. Even if it seems like it will be impossible to sit by your pet's side as you say goodbye for the very last time, try to muster up the courage. If we think about our own passing from this world, it's a hope for many of us to be surrounded by people who love us as we breathe our last breath. While it is not common, you may find your pet is trying to isolate themselves to die alone. If this happens to you, take comfort in knowing this is how nature programmed animals— to leave their herd at the end of life so as not to risk predators coming in and attacking the herd while they're weak.

When the vet showed up for Samson's appointment, things went relatively quickly, which makes sense because most appointments are scheduled for an hour, inclusive of transporting the body to the vet's vehicle if you opt for cremation. The vet walked us through everything in real time, but it might be helpful to know exactly what to prepare for in case you don't get a play by play. Two drugs are administered; the first puts your pet into a deep sleep while the second stops the heart. The vet warned us there could be some fluid loss (pee or poo) at the time of death, and/or the tongue might roll out of the mouth in an unexpected way. Those things didn't happen with Samson, but it was nice to know that it was a totally normal possibility, and we shouldn't be alarmed.

I do wish I'd taken a video of the thirty-minute-long process so I could watch it again later, as it's all such a blur. I don't know if I would keep the video for the long-term, but I wish I had the option today to relive it just once. I definitely wish I'd gotten Murphy on video when Samson's spirit communicated to him from the ceiling above where Samson's body lay. If I were to do it again, I would set up my phone on a tripod or prop it up against a book and leave the video camera rolling so I wouldn't have to actively think about it in real time.

I also wish I'd thought to ask some departed loved ones, guides, or other special pets in spirit to meet Samson as he crossed over. I know now that Samson's first dad and my sister's dog Cooper were there to greet him, which is comforting. I could have requested a huge reception for him from my spirit guides!

Finally, another thing I hadn't been prepared for was the exact moment of death. I could feel the energy shift. There was a lightness

I'd never experienced before. I recently read a book called *Journey of Souls*, and I generally agree with the journey it describes—a transitioned soul departs their earthly body and can look down on the scene from above. They can still hear and see everyone, though they feel an incredible freedom. I believe our animals hang around full-time for two to three months after they pass, largely to make sure we're okay and to complete their transition. During this time, they might send signs, and it may be normal to frequently sense their presence. I like to think of this as a magical part of the experience.

Chapter 5

MORE OF THE MAGIC, PLEASE!

The majority of our pets decide on a general timeline to cross over and leave their bodies behind. I believe when our pets choose to cross over, there's a higher-order reason for it, or, put more simply, they've accomplished what they came here for. I'm referring to a "soul contract," which is a life goal or lesson a person or pet agrees to work on or accomplish before they jump into a new life. Both people and animals are born with pre-existing soul contracts they've already signed up for. I think of these informal contracts as promises we make to ourselves or to others, and once complete, a soul may decide to go on to the next phase of their journey.

One of my animal communicator friends recounted a very sad story in which one of her client's dogs jumped out of a bike basket to a tragic death. The dog's mom didn't know that she herself was pregnant at the time, and in hindsight, she doesn't know how she would have been able to raise her child as a single mom if she'd had a dog as well. She takes comfort in knowing that her dog knew it was time to leave her, and while we never want an accident or any traumatic event to take our pets from us, it's nice to know that our pets are connected to the universe in mysterious and magical ways. They are always here for us, even when they transition from this world.

Reincarnation

Simply stated, reincarnation is defined as "the rebirth of a soul in a new body." The spectrum of beliefs on reincarnation ranges from "it definitely doesn't exist" to "it definitely does exist." On the "it does exist" side, there are a few schools of thoughts on how it happens and other rules that govern the process. From my own experience and the extensive research and many animal communication readings I've done, I believe reincarnation is very real, and it's one of the most magical things we can experience with our pets.

Back to the *Journey of Souls* book that was briefly discussed in chapter 4. It argues that once we leave our body at the time of transition (death), our soul stays in close proximity to our living loved ones. As mentioned, I think animals stick around for a few months this way. After that, Dr. Newton, the author of the book, describes how souls return to "heaven" and go through a formal process to review their life on Earth with one of their teachers. Then they are re-routed back to their heavenly home. This home consists of a large cluster of souls, and within that is a smaller group of five to six souls. He calls this smaller group a "soul family." The book is quite fascinating, as Dr. Newton describes actual conversations he has had with clients in deep hypnosis who recount their experience of their "life between lives."

Dr. Newton's research reveals we have predetermined soul contracts prior to entering each life. I believe the same is true for animals that are pets: they have predetermined soul contracts that they will fulfill with their pet parents (humans). I also believe the soul families that many clients describe to Dr. Newton can include animal souls. While researching pet loss grief, I heard many people refer to their crossed-over pet as a "soul dog" or "soul cat." I totally get it because this is how I think of Samson. It makes perfect sense to me that animal souls would cross paths with us in multiple lives, just like we see in the 2017 film *A Dog's Purpose*. While all dogs are special, and we'll mourn each one, there are extra special ones that hurt even more. I believe this is because we've had many past lives with them, and our souls are bonded together closely.

Some animal communicators will tell you that reincarnation has to be written in the cosmos for it to happen. I don't believe that. I believe if you want your dog to come back to you, they will try. It might be a pure reincarnation where the complete soul of your passed pet is in the new body of a future pet. Or it might be that aspects of the soul of your passed pet are in the new body as a guide for another soul. Regardless of which reincarnation process you experience, the new pet will not be a clone of the last one. You'll see lots of similarities and feel the same energy buzz due to the soul connection. But it won't be exactly the same, just like a human soul won't be exactly the same in its next incarnation.

Animals prefer to wait until their humans are through the grief process and mostly healed before they come back in a new body. I know this because Samson told me. I had one of the coolest animal communication downloads (spiritual transmissions) I've experienced on July 10, about eight weeks after Samson died. I was deep in the grieving process, and I wasn't sleeping well. At around midnight, as I was spinning in my despair, I felt a calm presence right beside me.

SAMSON'S STORY

Two calm presences, in fact. I sensed Samson just to the right of me and my nephew, Cooper, my sister's chocolate Lab, who passed away three years ago, just to my left. Samson started talking to me so clearly that I grabbed my phone and took these notes as he spoke:

> It was my time to go.
> The way in which I died doesn't matter. Please don't be guilty.
> You have to focus on gratitude and remembering the good times.
> I have to help you heal so I can come back.
> Lilly will be with me.
> You have to watch for us online because others will try to adopt us.
> Someone you know will adopt Lilly.
> We will look like Samson did.
> I'm with Cooper now.
> Cooper and my first dad were there when I crossed over.
> I am happy and having fun.
> I don't want to see you upset.

I told him I wished I could hug him.

> I still feel you and so I don't really miss you per se.
> It's very different here but very good.
> You need to lean into the soul resonance and frequency.
> You have to eliminate anything negative in your life and increase your vibration.
> You are meant to help thousands of dogs.
> Part of our story is to help make people aware of the drug Librela.

In the last chapter, I'll share more on Librela and how I figured out that this shot for arthritis he received in November 2023 may have contributed to his declining health.

> You weren't ready to know about it, which is why you didn't connect the dots till much later.
> I didn't suffer, Mommy.
> Our bodies want high-resonating frequency, and this drug is low frequency—some can change it, and some can't.
> More dogs and cats than are supposed to will be harmed from it so we do need to sound the alarm.
> I've already gotten some things done mommy, but it's been harder on you than I imagined.

Before he died, I sensed that Samson wanted to help his second family with some things, and I believe that is what he'd been working on.

> I keep sending you signs.
> I'm glad when you see them, like how you watched *The River Wild* movie with the main character's name being Gail and she had a yellow Lab!
> I try to send yellow Labs your way all the time.

Yes, you do, my boy. I see them often and smile.

> Your frequency matches dog frequency, Mom. That's why dogs are so attracted to you.
> It's pure energy, and it's light energy, and it's love.
> You have a huge capacity for love, and I was here to teach you how to tap into it.
> My next time here, we will go up a level in our work to help people.
> I am excited for my next life.
> It's a good one.
> I wouldn't miss being with you, Mommy.

> It's time where we will be together for a lot of these lives because we have work to do to help others.
> When you are writing the book and can't think of something, close your eyes, and I'll help you.

I do believe you've written a good amount of this book, sweet Samson!

> Murphy is helping too. He is evolving.

This one made me laugh out loud.

> I've been helping Murphy where possible.
> I'm excited for Honey Snow, and I think it will be good for him.

Honey Snow was a foster dog we were scheduled to pick up a few days later.

> He will have a few falters but overall will be successful with her.
> Once you start a morning ritual, your power will be unstoppable.
> And animals have always been your calling.
> You are finally waking up to that in this life.
> It will be a very rewarding and meaningful next chapter for you.
> Follow your heart about what to focus on.
> Things will come to you as you need to know them.
> I love you, my world, Mommy.
> I love Daddy too, but Daddy's dog is coming soon.
> You will have three, Mommy.
> Murph belongs to both.
> I will always be Mommy's boy.
> I don't think I come as a girl next time, but it's never for sure.

You'll start to hear another name right before you find me, and you'll know it's getting close.
Some woman is involved, probably who posts about us.
I can help more here than when I was alive.
I do miss Milk-Bones.

Another good laugh.

Mommy, you have to help people with the grief.
It is debilitating for so many.
Follow your heart.
Speak from the heart.
People will listen and follow your lead.
They are lost after their pet dies.
And some pets don't know how to help them.
But the dogs and cats are always around for as long as the person needs and asks.

If Samson says it, it must be true! You can always ask your pet for help.

People should always talk to their pets.
Reincarnation is written in the cards.
We have multiple lives mapped out at a time.
We are helpers.
We often work with the same people.
Sometimes our people are connected to each other and sometimes not at all.
It's like an assignment at one point, but later we can choose.
And we often follow where we feel the most love.
This is why love conquers all and leads people where they need to go.

This makes so much sense. If we send our dogs love, the chances they stay with us and consider coming back are much higher.

> Love is how you talk to Zoetis (the maker of Librela).
> No mean words, only love words.
> Cooper is like the head farmer; he is a supervisor.
> He helps you get dog souls on their journey.

And then we transitioned to Cooper, which was quite a stark contrast from Samson. I saw images from Cooper, whereas Samson's communication comes in words and a general sense of knowing.

I got some messages for my sister, as Cooper was her chocolate Lab. He told me he sent her the two dogs and two cats she has adopted since his passing. He also showed me a stunning display of gold and silver polka dots, shimmering in midair. I got the feeling I was supposed to tell Laura to watch for a sign from Cooper that involves polka dots. He also showed me two images very clearly. The first was of him on a lifeguard stand out in a farm field, where he seemed to be supervising others. He was wearing a royal blue ball cap and had a whistle in his mouth. The other image was of my sister's last apartment. Cooper was lying on the middle of the living room floor, and lots of sunshine was pouring in. He was looking my way and smiling. I sensed that he had many good memories there. (When I relayed these images to my sister, she chuckled and said she used to call Cooper a referee and that he'd shown me his favorite spot to lie in the apartment. She is still anxiously awaiting the polka dot message.) And then just as quickly as the download had turned to Cooper, we turned back to Samson.

> Daddy gets sad and doesn't know what to say so he lets you do the talking, Mommy.

> He is supportive, which is good.
> I would hope he can sing songs about me and listen to more music because that helps Daddy.
> And to play with Murphy.
> Murphy knows when I'm here, but it's not like he sees me.
> He just senses me and knows it like clairsentience.
> Pastel colors are good for you right now.
> Once you start communicating with dogs again, that will help.
> You should try the podcast for animal communications.
> You should build a platform for both dogs' and peoples' voices.
> Do research on what is out there and define what you want and go for it.
> The book will be fast to publish.
> It will sell out.

My sweet optimistic boy. ☺

> You will go on tour, and I will come with you.
> It will be fun.
> Dad and Murphy and the other dog, which is a girl, will come too.
> Your third foster dog you'll keep.

And with that little mic drop at the end, Samson and Cooper left. If you feel like this download was all over the place, that's precisely how animal communications typically happen. You get insightful nuggets interspersed with fun, funny, sweet, and random thoughts.

If we pull out the reincarnation tidbits, Samson describes it both as an assignment but also as something that can be chosen. Even more importantly, he shares that dogs will reincarnate where they feel a lot of love. Before he passed away, I asked Samson if he was planning to come back to me. He said yes, in about six months, I would find him online and he will be a small to medium-size, yellow-whitish puppy alongside one of his siblings. He told me in this download that the sibling would be named Lilly, which is a name I have heard many times this summer and already knew it would have some significance in Samson's next chapter.

I've learned that names are important signs, as I heard the name Samson multiple times before I fostered him. And then I heard the name Murphy for over a year before we found him. I knew Murphy would be reincarnated from a former dog my family had named Elwood. I knew what colors he would be (Doberman colors but not a Doberman), where he would be (north of Chicago, in a litter of puppies), and when I'd find him (just past Christmastime). But when I finally found him, I was still unsure.

The day Murphy's foster parents brought him to our house, I heard clear as day in my mind "familiar names are important." The foster parents were rattling off many familiar names of pets that I knew. For example, the first dog adopted from Murphy's litter was renamed Cooper by his new family. I asked the foster parents if they happened to know a dog named Elwood. They said no, but their neighbor's son was named Elwood. Whoa. Elwood is a unique name, and I'd chosen it because the other black Lab we had at the time was named Jake—a la the Blues Brothers.

Murphy's first day with us.

Despite hearing lots of familiar names, one of which was Elwood, I asked the universe for a bigger sign to show me that Murphy was really Elwood reincarnated. A few days later, I was picking up some antique nightstands from a house about fifteen miles north of where I live. When I arrived, the gal who met me said I could look through the house and make an offer on any other items I liked. I saw a cool antique chair with a pink embroidered seat and turned it over—it said Norma, the name of my grandma. I found a nice vintage clock and opened the back of it to see if it had a year like some older wares often do. I couldn't believe it. Right inside that clock, it said Elwood. I laughed out loud. I bought the clock. And then on my drive home, when I called my sister with the news of a sign I could finally believe, we realized that it was April 22nd, Elwood's birthday.

Communicating with Your Animal

You've probably realized by now that I have a unique gift: the ability to communicate with animals. Some of you may think I'm crazy, and that's okay. I think it's a bit crazy too, but my communications have unearthed so many correct things I could never have otherwise known that I have to just trust it! I learned I could do this about five years ago. I happened upon a video of a black leopard in South Africa that had been abused in a zoo in Europe earlier in its life. An animal communicator worked with this large cat named Diabolo (Spanish for Devil) and learned that the animal wanted a new name, requesting to be called Spirit. Once the name was changed and this animal communicator did some healing work with Spirit, his behavior transformed. I had never heard of animal communication before, but I wanted to try it. So I found an instructor on Udemy named Claire Bloomfield and took a few of her classes, spending a total of about $100.

SAMSON'S STORY

Anyone can talk with animals, though I believe it's hardest to connect with your own pets. I do find it much easier to connect with Samson now that he is no longer in his Earthly body. The basics of animal communication include getting into a meditative state and then telepathically conversing with an animal, assuming you have the pet parent's permission to do so. My method starts with grounding and setting an intention that the experience is protected by white light and done for the highest good of the animal. I then look at a picture of the animal where I can clearly see their eyes, and I start the conversation. Some people might hear, see, feel, or just know information once they open lines of communication. I find that it varies for me based on the way the animal likes to communicate. We saw in the example with Samson and Cooper that Samson is more auditory, and Cooper is more visual.

There are tons of ways to connect with animals in order to communicate with them. You might try a few methods on your own or take a class if it sounds up your alley. Another option is to pay an animal communicator for a session (Mary Helen and Jaime's websites are https://www.itsmynature-mhs.com and https://jaimebreeze.com if you'd like to look them up). Over the years, I've had six different animal communicators talk with my pets. They each bring a unique flavor and talent, and all have been helpful. If you're looking to connect with your pet in the afterlife, I would search for someone who specializes in talking with animals in spirit. You could also find a communicator who is well versed in reincarnation, if that is something you want to explore. Animal communication sessions range from $100 to $500 per hour, with the majority being about $150. If you decide to book a session, you'll want to identify some questions ahead of time to make sure you use the time wisely. I typically ask the communicator to spend thirty minutes with each of my dogs, and

I have at least eight questions prepared for each dog, as sometimes the answers will come in quite fast, and you can get through a lot of material.

Interpreting animal communication is an art because animals will express their thoughts and feelings in unusual ways. Sometimes things won't make any sense, such as when Samson shared that death is like a flock of birds that is there and then all of a sudden gone. I just thought he was being wise Samson, and that he didn't mean anything specific—until after his euthanasia appointment, when the vet told us the story of the big flock of birds flying out of a tree at the exact moment a dog's heart stopped. Then I knew it had been a sign.

The cool thing about animals is they're generally more connected and more psychic than we are. This is how they know things that might occur in the future. They can also make things happen, such as Samson sending us a third foster with a bird name. He may very well have been at the shelter in Missouri and whispered the name Lark in the ear of the person who named her. He then somehow guided her on a transport and made sure we were the fosters that picked her up that day. More on Lark in the last chapter!

Some parts of your animal communication reading might seem incorrect. For example, one time a dog told me he didn't have any pet siblings in the house. His mom told me that was false, but he did avoid them at all costs. The dog told me no, because in his lived experience he didn't have any furry siblings because he was never around them. Dogs share information the way they see it, which might not match our reality or how we would describe something. They can bring up information from the past. For example, Samson showed a communicator an armchair that seemed important to him, but we do not have one. I believe it was connected to his first Dad, who had passed away, which led to Samson's intake at the Chicagoland Lab Rescue, where his second family, and ultimately, I, would adopt him.

In my experiences talking with animals and paying animal communicators to talk with my pets, I think there are some universal truths that might be helpful to know:

1. Animals are almost always joyful and positive, and they do not hold grudges, nor do they want to discuss painful things. If you feel any guilt at all over the loss of your pet, please know they forgive you 110 percent. They never, ever, blame their parent in any way, even if they died in a traumatic accident.
2. Animals like to be around us once they pass away. As I've mentioned, I think they stick around all the time for at least a few months, and after that, they come and go. So your pet may still be with you! Some, but not all, will send signs. You can tap into your pet's energy through a mindfulness activity (meditation, journaling, a walk in nature, etc.)
3. Animals love to talk about themselves, and well, about everything! I have never had an animal that was not interested in talking. Usually when I introduce myself and ask if they'd like to talk, I get an enthusiastic, "Sure!" One time, I saw a dog get so excited he spun around like the Tasmanian Devil, then he put his front paws out to each side like he was shooting two invisible guns and said, "Suns out, guns out!" You can't make this stuff up. This dog definitely had one of the more memorable personalities from my readings!
4. Animals don't miss us like we miss them. Samson's response when I told him I wanted to hug him is indicative of this. They're still with us, so they don't really feel like much has changed.

5. They do worry about us and want us to be happy. They hate more than anything to see us sad, depressed, and blaming ourselves for their death. They want us to remember good times, as they pick up our energy frequencies. The happier we are, the happier they are. They need us to be coming out of the grief tunnel before they can come back to us, if that is their plan.
6. Animals can hear us talk to them. They love to hear our voices. And they love to feel our love. In fact, you can send them love even when they're not here. You might imagine a beam of light coming out of your heart and going into theirs, just like the old Care Bear stare. If you don't know what I'm talking about, Google it. ☺
7. They can help us with things from the other side. All we have to do is ask for their assistance. I've asked Samson many times to help Murphy with his behavior issues. And I think he has!
8. When we love other animals who are still here in body, our departed animals can feel that love. This is why we might consider getting another pet if we only have one. I still had Murphy after Samson was gone, but it wasn't until we started fostering and had two dogs around that I could get to a dog love quotient that was closer to normal for me.

I always take notes or make a voice recording (with permission) of an animal communication session I pay for so that I can revisit it later and see if anything makes sense with more history under my belt. I find animal communication sessions to be not only informative about how my dog is feeling, but also very insightful in general about how they think and what's important to them. If you are curious at all about animal communication, why not book a session or take a class? The worst thing that can happen is that it doesn't work. But I think there's a high likelihood you'll experience some magical synchronicities or messages.

SAMSON'S STORY

Even if you don't believe in animal communication, a pet's soul sticking around after they pass, or reincarnation, some of what I've written in this chapter may still be helpful for you as you go through the grieving process. For example, sending love to your passed animal may make you feel metaphorically closer to them, even if you don't believe they're physically around in spirit. Talking out loud to them, journaling about them, singing them songs, writing them letters, or meditating in their favorite place in your house might be comforting.

If you wish something magical would happen to you, set that intention, and you never know what might happen. For example, I could say:

> Dear Samson, I hope you're still here, and I would love to see a sign from you if you can please send one. I'm feeling sad right now and trying to get better. I would love for you to give me strength and help me know how to get through this. I'll be paying attention if you have any messages or ideas for me. P.S.—Please help your brother Murphy who is acting out a bit now that you're gone.

Try this every day for a few weeks and see what happens. Does something inspirational pop into your head? Do you keep hearing a song over and over that seems to be a message from your pet? Does anything weird but cool happen to you? Are there things that keep reminding you of your pet? I'm a big believer that if we ask, our pets will listen, and we're all capable of experiencing magic if we seek it out.

Chapter 6

DEALING WITH GRIEF AND GUILT

It took me about three months of grieving, energy work, self-reflection, crying, talking about it, and writing about it to get to the point where I felt even remotely qualified to talk about the topics of grief and guilt. This chapter includes some background information that I found helpful on my own journey as well as learnings from the survey I conducted. Remember, there's no single correct way to process pet loss grief. You should do what feels right for you, and I hope you find some meaningful ways to honor yourself and your pet during this time.

Losing a Pet May Be Harder Than Losing a Person

Three days after Samson died, one of my high school friends happened to post a Ted Talk about pet loss grief given by emergency veterinarian Sarah Hoggan. This was one of the most helpful resources I stumbled across. In the Ted Talk, Dr. Hoggan says our grief is real because the emotions we had with our pets were real, and she reminds us that grief is a documented medical condition with real symptoms including crying, insomnia, fatigue, confusion, and a feeling of profound sadness.

She says it's not only normal to grieve, but it's also normal to relive every minute and every decision we made at the end of their lives. "We are hardwired to recognize pain as a teacher ... that means we need to study the events that lead to the pain so we can avoid it in the future." It's totally normal that we replay the events that occurred at the end of their life again and again and again. Even just knowing this fact helped me to recognize and understand why I was doing it and to find grace for myself when the replays turned on in my mind.

Dr. Hoggan's patients consistently report they feel different (and often worse) when losing a pet versus losing a person. Dr. Hoggan points to three things that drive this difference, which I expand on below:

1. Our society diminishes the validity of pet loss pain, saying it's not as important as losing a person. This introduces shame, isolation, and additional agony when we lose a pet because we feel we have to grieve on our own.
2. The relationship with pets is different—they do not judge us but rather love us unconditionally. A pet's love is one of the purest forms of love, which could make the hurt even stronger.
3. Pets cannot tell us they're tired and ready to go. We have to make their decisions for them, and they are 100 percent dependent on us. It's similar to losing a child who is still very young or has special needs, which are very traumatic losses as well.

Beyond these three differences, Dr. Hoggan shares that comorbidities can make the pet loss feel even worse. She points to five common comorbidities:

1. You lost your pet or had to make a euthanasia decision because of a preventable accident. It is normal to blame yourself when this happens, but no one can predict every single thing that could go wrong in a pet's life.
2. Your pet was a "broken soul" rescue who learned to love again when you saved them, creating a very special bond. Dr. Hoggan assures, "Your first rescue brought them joy. Your second rescue gave them peace." This one is a real tearjerker for me.
3. Your dog rescued you during a tough time in your life, devoting their life to you when you needed it most. I identify most with this comorbidity as it relates to Samson's passing. He helped me through the season of my life when I remembered and processed a lot of my own past trauma.
4. Your pet was a link to a lost loved one, and it hurts doubly hard when you lose your treasured pet as you relive that first loss as well.
5. Your pet is more than a pet because they're your service companion and help you get through the routine tasks of your day.

We can't just "get over" the loss of a pet. We can't just replace a pet when they die. When society in general or individuals we know tell us this through their words, looks, or actions, they are 100 percent wrong. We have to allow ourselves to grieve, because the emotions are real.

The Stages of Grief

Currently, there are five widely accepted stages of grief, based on the Kübler-Ross Model, which was introduced by Elisabeth Kübler-Ross in her 1969 book, *On Death and Dying*:

1. Denial—a defense mechanism that deadens some of the shock of the transition you face. You likely will utter the word "No" often when this phase rears its head. "No way this has happened." "No, no, no, it can't be."
2. Anger—a mask that helps us hide from the pain and emotion of the loss. With pet loss, we can take our anger out on the disease, accident, veterinarian, and many times, ourselves. We place blame and spin on it in circles, again and again, to avoid processing our feelings.
3. Bargaining—a phase where we grasp at straws, hoping to regain some control over the terrible predicament we find ourselves in. These "if only" statements sneak into our minds when something reminds of us our pet, and we wish we could do anything to have them back. Or we know they're dying, and we offer ideas to the universe to change the path forward. "What if I never leave their side, then will my pet live?"
4. Depression—there is a heaviness when we finally sit in the emotion of the loss. It can be a sad and isolating stage when we get to depression, and this is often the hardest stage for many people to process. It may be helpful to consider assistance from a mental health professional if you remain withdrawn from life for a prolonged period of time.
5. Acceptance—the light peeks through the end of the tunnel in this stage, as we can honestly say we understand what has occurred. And while we don't like it, we have come to accept a new way of life, and we're putting one foot in front of the other with more good days than bad ones.

The denial phase was relatively swift for me after Samson died, as I had two and a half weeks leading up to his death to prepare for it. It probably lasted for one to two weeks following his passing.

I can imagine that an accidental and/or unexpected death with no advanced warning might result in a longer and more intense denial period.

The anger and bargaining phases were intertwined for me, as both tend to be quite active coping mechanisms. I found myself reliving all the events of the past few years related to Samson's health, especially vet trips. What did I do right? What did I do wrong? What did the vets do right? What did the vets do wrong? Where did I see cracks that might warrant some blame as I tried to understand how this could have happened? On the flipside, any little thing that reminded me of Samson would trigger the bargaining. I passed a dog park where I took Samson to meet my sister and her three dogs on Christmas in 2017, and I wished to go back to that day. "If only I can go back, then I would get to experience everything with him all over again." I even found myself wanting to go back and relive bad experiences in my life if it meant I would get to have Samson again. Anger and bargaining came and went for about six weeks or so for me.

Next was a heavy depression. I was in a very sad place for three to four weeks. Lots of guttural crying, sometimes accompanied with what felt like full-body convulsions. I was numb and just going through the motions of everyday life. I could tell I wasn't my usual happy self, as I didn't feel like there was any reason to be overly positive about life. I didn't care about much. Honestly, the only thing that pulled me out of this funk was fostering dogs. When Samson came to me in the middle of the night on July 10, he told me, "This has been much harder on you than I could have imagined." I was squarely in the depression stage at that point. As you'll read in the last chapter, I believe he handpicked Lark to send our way because he knew we'd adopt her, and he knew she'd counteract my depression. And he was right!

SAMSON'S STORY

As I write this book, now three months since Samson's passing, I believe I've reached some kind of acceptance. It's getting easier to talk about the good memories, and it's less often that I think of the pain and anguish we suffered at the end of his life.

It's common for these five stages of grief to pop up out of order and after you think you've "completed" them. Some say grief is a circle, and you never know when or where you'll get pulled back to the circle. I also think of grief as leaving a hole in your heart that is irreversible, but the heart will grow because of the love you had for your pet and the love you'll have for new pets. So while that hole may always be there, the heart gets larger and larger, making the hole relatively smaller and hurting less and less. It's also important to remember that some people can get through the grief process in a few days, while others might take years. Some believe we never truly complete the grieving process but rather integrate it into our lives. The survey I did among 121 pet parents suggests the average grief duration when losing a pet is approximately thirteen months.

In 2019, David Kessler teamed up with Elisabeth Kübler-Ross to write a book about a sixth stage of grief: finding meaning. This stage is all about honoring the legacy of the person or pet we lost. We can't bring them back, so the world we knew is forever gone. But we can rebuild a world going forward where we integrate their memory and essence in a way that allows us (and them) further healing. I think this is a beautiful step in the grieving process, and one we'll touch on in the next chapter.

Grieving More Than Just Your Pet

In addition to grieving the physical loss of our pet, there can be other things we need to grieve. For example, my husband and I had to acknowledge that we'd put parts of our lives on hold to be caretakers for Samson during his final years and especially in his final weeks. Just like a caregiver of a child with special needs or of an aging parent knows, you have to learn a new way of life once the person or animal you've been taking care of leaves this Earth.

I also had to come to terms with all of the things I'd planned to do with or for my boy Samson. We never got around to getting him a concrete driveway in Tennessee so that he wouldn't have to hurt his paws on the gravel. We didn't get to visit with Matt's parents so that his Grandma and Grandpa could see him before he passed away. We had wanted to take him on more trips to explore Tennessee, and I was hoping to take him on a road trip out west to explore Montana and Wyoming. Sadly, we ran out of time. I have to mourn that I had plans and hopes and dreams that will never happen, and that's okay.

Grief May Be Different with Each Animal

While this was my first pet loss, I hear from others that it sometimes changes from pet to pet. I suppose this makes sense, but it's a good reminder, nonetheless.

> People should know that every death is different and the way you grieved a previous pet may have been an entirely different experience. Also, there is no timeline and no fast way to make it stop. Grief is grief. It takes as long as it takes. The only way out if it is to experience it fully without apology. Grief is not a mental illness. It's not depression. It's a normal reaction to the loss of a loved one.
>
> —*Survey respondent*

SAMSON'S STORY

Acknowledging and Overcoming Guilt

Another aspect of grief we must discuss is guilt. It is sometimes listed among seven stages of grief, but I like the list of six above, and I feel guilt is more polarizing, as it sometimes accompanies grief, but sometimes does not at all.

A whopping 71 percent of the 121 survey respondents felt some guilt around the death of their pet. 51 percent of all respondents experienced guilt about their role as caregiver and the treatment decisions they made for their pet. They wish they'd seen signs of the illness sooner; they feel like they generally let their pet down and couldn't save them; and they wish they'd questioned the vet more and done further research about the care that was given.

> I didn't recognize Cooper was getting weaker before the sudden death. On that night, we couldn't get to the vet because it was a holiday weekend, and the emergency vet is over an hour away. I feel bad I didn't do more that night, and I didn't recognize he was failing in the days beforehand.
> —*Survey respondent*

> Mackey had a cough we all just thought was allergies, but it was likely the lymphoma that was the unfortunate diagnosis. We wish we'd caught it sooner.
> —*Survey respondent*

> If I had more monies / funds maybe I could have more aggressively treated my cat's urinary problems. I also could have maybe attempted a rehoming to someone who had more ability to do medication more intensely.
> —*Survey respondent*

We thought Lilly's limping on her paw was due to an arthritis flareup. She was diagnosed with arthritis at the young age of three, and we had been controlling it with medication. Every once in a while, she would have a flareup and need additional medication. So she was limping, and we did pen rest and ice and tried to let it heal without going to the vet. After two weeks, we went to the vet, and they took an X-ray of her wrist and saw that the arthritis was worse, gave us stronger medication, and we went home. After two weeks of no improvement, we went back and did X-rays of her shoulder and found out she had bone cancer. We got her leg amputated the following week. She had a super aggressive form of bone cancer, but we always wonder if we'd caught it a month sooner if the chemo would've made a difference.

—*Survey respondent*

I strongly believe that the annual vaccinations and monthly flea & heartworm treatments along with the recommended food had a big part to play in Maurice's lymphoma. I blame myself for trusting our then vet and the pet food industry.

—*Survey respondent*

While only 3 percent of respondents lost a pet to a traumatic event or accident, I want to touch on this topic, as I can imagine it's especially hard to lose a pet this way. If you are a pet owner who has lived through this, I am so sorry. I think back to Dr. Sarah Hoggan's Ted Talk where she shared that one of her patients lost a puppy who ate a container full of chemo medicine. Chemotherapy drugs are meant to kill fast-growing cells, and a puppy is nothing but fast growing cells, so there was no hope. The dog parent was distraught over having left the cream out on the nightstand where the pup grabbed it. Dr. Hoggan reminds us that there is no way we can account for all potential accidents at all times, and we have to forgive ourselves when an accident unfortunately happens.

> Odin and his brother Loki were primarily indoor cats, but when we moved out of the city, I liked to let them out on the porch to feel the breeze and hear the birds. Odin busted out of the screen to hunt in the woods and was attacked by a fisher cat. It was my job to protect him, and I didn't.
> —*Survey respondent*

If you have lost a pet due to a tragic accident, you might be even more likely to experience post-traumatic stress disorder. My research on this suggests you might try specific therapies such as EMDR or tapping to help reset your nervous system, which is replaying and reacting to the traumatic memories on loop. Basic introductions can be found at www.emdria.org and thetappingsolution.com, or you can look for guided sessions on YouTube.

One other resource to consider is the Pet Compassion Careline at 1-855-245-8214. I didn't try this, but a Reddit thread states, "I wasn't sure of it at first...but I tried it, and I'm so glad I did. It's completely free, and calling the number connects you directly to a certified counselor who's just there to help, listen, and give comfort specifically regarding the passing of a beloved pet. No strings attached, just seems to be a genuinely altruistic thing. I've called twice (they said calling multiple times was completely fine), and both calls lasted about 15 mins. The woman I talked to was so kind and empathetic."

21 percent of survey respondents felt guilty about the euthanasia decision, including if they did it too soon or too late, and just that they did it at all:

Not sure if I made the right decision letting Cara go. Should've been more vocal to the vet about every symptom she was experiencing. Should've done more to figure out what was causing all her symptoms."

—Survey respondent

I took Drake to the vet because he couldn't keep food down or hold most of his bowel movements. When we got to the vet, they said he was severely dehydrated. The vet suggested putting him down, or I could come back. I knew I would never be able to bring him back. However, after I agreed to put him down, I regretted not taking another week to do all his favorite things. I still regret it, but I know he was in pain.

—Survey respondent

We decided on euthanasia because Hoops was anemic, getting extremely weak and wouldn't eat. Even though it likely spared him pain and suffering, I felt guilty for making that choice, like I was the one who killed him, not the cancer.

—Survey respondent

I felt like we murdered Gilly by putting her down and that we were responsible for her death.

—Survey respondent

A few of the survey respondents didn't or weren't able to euthanize but wish they had:

I felt guilt about whether there was anything more I could have done, both to treat his cancer earlier and to euthanize him at the end. We discovered his lymphoma shortly after his annual check-up, and I second-guessed myself about whether I should have moved his annual checkup date up to catch and treat it earlier. I also didn't realize how rapidly his lymphoma had advanced: From the time he was tentatively diagnosed to the time he died was three weeks. I took Baxter to the vet three days before he died, and they told me he likely had lymphoma, but didn't signal he was approaching death. He ended up convulsing at 11 p.m. and dying in my arms on the way to the Medvet emergency vet. I felt really guilty about him suffering through this, and angry at my regular vet for not being more transparent about the severity of Baxter's condition.

—Survey respondent

One person even shared a powerful example of how we can regret and feel guilty about a very specific thing we did or didn't do during the euthanasia process.

We put our cat Sabbath to sleep, and I wish I'd given him his favorite thing in the world—the water from a can of tuna ... I'm crying writing this.

—Survey respondent

15 percent of the survey respondents indicated they had experienced guilt because they wish they'd spent more quality time with their pet. They lament not having done more of the things their pet loved, and those who weren't able to physically be there for their pet at the end wish they had been:

I wish I had spent more time with Tre in his last months, given him more of the food and experiences he loved.

—Survey respondent

A lot of the guilt I hold is that I didn't stay with my cat during his final moments. I was a young mom with two kids and felt so awful that he kept having these troubles and felt like it was my fault and that I had given up on him.

—*Survey respondent*

I was traveling so much for work and wasn't home much the last year of Luca's life. He passed while I was gone. I found him curled up near the door when I got home after working a 16-hour day.

—*Survey respondent*

If you're one of the many people who experience guilt about the passing of your pet for any reason, please try to forgive yourself. Your pet does not blame you, and they definitely do not want you to blame yourself. Just know that it's a normal part of the process if you do feel guilt, and the faster you can move through it and leave it behind you, the better.

I wish I had not gone down that awful guilt path. It was unwarranted and was pure torture.

—*Survey respondent*

Chapter 7

WHAT TO DO AFTER YOUR PET PASSES

This chapter examines tangible things you can do as you grieve the loss of your pet.

It's helpful to first review the 121-person survey results regarding grief. 43 percent of respondents reported that honoring their passed pet was the number one way to heal in the grieving process. They experienced healing through sharing stories and looking at photos and videos of their pet, making and displaying memorials such as an urn of ashes or special items in the home, talking with others about their pet, and looking for signs they're still around.

> My girls painted an urn for Tre's ashes. It sits on our mantle and I talk to it, hold it. I still say hi to him when I enter a room where he would usually have been. We tell a lot of stories about him and always reference when something happens that he would have loved or how he would have reacted. I also believe he came back to life as a hawk (weird, I know)—but a hawk landed outside our house the morning after he died and just walked around on the sidewalk. Then it landed in the top of a tree and just watched us.

It has also flown past my car a few times while driving. I love seeing him as the hawk; it helps me feel like Tre is with us.
—Survey respondent

I hung my favorite photos of Ralph in my house so I could see him everyday at his happiest.
—Survey respondent

I started a canine rehab business in honor of Meena.
—Survey respondent

It's been 3.5 years. Drake's pictures are still up. My phone screen saver is still him. My dad still puts fresh dirt and flowers on his burial spot. I think that helps me remember him.
—Survey respondent

We will be scattering Daisy's ashes at a peaceful beach that we can visit in the future and will always remind us of her life.
—Survey respondent

I feel like most of the time, everyone around you just expects you to 'get over it' after a few weeks at most. It's really hard having to mask my grief every day. I still wear my heart necklace that has some of her ashes in it every day. I still think about her all the time. I still cry about her all the time. I'm still grieving, and it's been over a year. It doesn't feel like I'll ever be 'over it' if I'm honest. She was my everything. I think a lot of people just don't understand how strong of a bond you can form with a pet.
—Survey respondent

One of the watchouts I read about in another book is to think twice before scattering all of your pet's ashes somewhere. It might be a good idea to keep at least a small amount of their ashes in a safe place, so you'll always have a physical remembrance of your pet going forward. I've also sadly heard about people who have lost their dogs' ashes in a fire, so you might think about putting some of their ashes in another location or in a fireproof safe if that feels right to you.

38 percent of respondents identified other animals as an integral part of their healing process. Some mentioned adopting or getting a new animal, while others focused on existing pets they already had. Fostering animals and volunteering at a local animal shelter were also helpful activities for some.

> Mackey was the oldest of our two dogs, and we actually thought it'd be a long time before we got a second dog again. Then, a rescue sort of found us, and we ended up adopting a second dog about four weeks later which really helped. I'm glad we didn't wait longer.
> —*Survey respondent*

> I adopted a puppy only a few months after losing my girl McCartney ... and I wish I'd given myself more time to process the grief. Raising a puppy while grieving was like a living hell.
> —*Survey respondent*

> I'm still healing, but Bailey sent me a new dog who I love.
> —*Survey respondent*

> I volunteered at an animal shelter and spent most of that time with cats, plus I would shower my friends' pets with love!
> —*Survey respondent*

21 percent of survey respondents leaned on support from other people, including loved ones, support groups, therapy, and social media chats.

> Hearing from others about their own experiences and them empathizing a lot with what I was going through was helpful. I assumed most people would think my emotions were wild because Mackey was "just a dog." But it turned out everyone had been through the same sort of emotions with their own pets.
> —*Survey respondent*

> My family and people closest to me IRL were completely unavailable and unsupportive. Strangers in a Pet Loss Facebook group were there for me.
> —*Survey respondent*

12 percent did self-care to heal, such as by reading and listening to grief experts, journaling, meditating, and crying freely.

> The book *Emotion Code* and energy work has had a profound effect on my younger dog after the loss of his pack leader. It has helped my own grief too.
> —*Survey respondent*

> Therapy but I'm still grieving deeply.
> —*Survey respondent*

> *The Grief Recovery Handbook* and meditation helped me.
> —*Survey respondent*

14 percent mentioned that nothing has helped them yet, and 14 percent said time is the best remedy. 3 percent stayed busy with work

or hobbies, and 6 percent found comfort in the end-of-life care decisions they'd made.

A friend shared the point that humans, when asked how they would want to die, generally say peacefully in their sleep—which is what we were providing our dog Snowy as his means of passing by putting him down. It also helped to remember that he wasn't at a point where he had suffered an injury from his age and conditions (like falling down stairs) that caused him acute pain. I have since watched people close to me let a pet suffer for a long time and feel comforted by the choice we made.
—*Survey respondent*

I'm glad we used an independent pet cremation service because we know we got Maurice back home with us.
—*Survey respondent*

Unlike the unprepared and slightly rushed vet office euthanasia of my dog from 10 years ago, this time I decided to have a home euthanasia for my kitty, and the entire process was just a million times better for everyone. The home visit vet was so kind and patient, and my kitty, Nuggzy, looked way more at ease and at peace than she would have been inside a vet office. The decision and process were still incredibly painful, but I was more able to find my composure, so that I could offer my kitty the support and love she deserved while she transitioned from this plane of existence to the next. I know not everyone can have this choice, but I hope home euthanasia becomes more accessible and affordable for every pet parent in the future.
—*Survey respondent*

40 percent respondents didn't know what they'd do differently during their grieving period. 19 percent wish they'd processed things differently, specifically by asking for help, forgiving themselves faster, and talking more openly about their loss. A few people wish they'd kept the ashes or asked for a paw print. One person mentioned they wish they'd held their dog longer before burying him. Three people wish they'd waited longer to adopt a new pet, while two said they should have adopted sooner. Two people said they should have minded their own health better, such as eating less sugar or drinking less alcohol.

> My ex buried Buddy. Next to the train tracks where he flushed out birds. I wish I would have gotten him cremated. I can't go visit his burial site because now it is far away and on private property. If I had him cremated, I would still have him.
>
> —*Survey respondent*

> I can't think of much I'd do differently. Since we knew Chuck was dying and had a limited range of time, we spent a lot of time celebrating him in his final year. His final year was also a good year, as he had cancer, but was also young and energetic. I was also a grad student and had the kind of schedule where I could sit in the park with him with a book in the afternoon or decide to take him outside for a few minutes just to share a snack and come back in. So much of my grief was front-loaded, which helped me feel like I had a lot in control.
>
> —*Survey respondent*

> I wish I hadn't been so angry; Fudge died because the vet pulled a catheter out and sent him home bleeding internally. There was nothing we could do when we found out, so it was a combination

SAMSON'S STORY

of rage and helplessness that would wash over me. I wish I spent more of that initial grieving time remembering the snuggles, endless reading, and loads of naps rather than cursing out some stupid animal hospital in Utah.

—*Survey respondent*

I processed my grief better this time than I did for my dog that died over 10 years ago, and the only thing I would have done differently is to ask for more help. While my kitty was getting sicker, I should have insisted on more help both in physical support and emotional/psychological support from the vet office(s) to people closest to me. Because dealing with the stress of vet visits, medication, research, and the emotional aspects of watching my beloved pet slowly decline made me feel so alone. I took on most of the responsibility when I should have found or demanded help from anywhere and everywhere.

—*Survey respondent*

Below are some specific ideas that might resonate with you as you work through the grief.

Take Care of Yourself

First and foremost, you must put yourself first after your pet is gone. This can be a really hard transition, especially if you had a period where your dog required a lot of palliative care. When Samson was gone, Matt and I felt lost. For years, we'd built a routine around him due to his limited mobility. We lifted him into the car, we took him with us nearly everywhere we went, and we went to more vet and rehab appointments than I care to admit. After an intensive caretaking journey, you may feel like your purpose for living is gone. If you're feeling this way, it's time to focus your caretaking inward.

Being as healthy as possible, spending time outdoors, and practicing whatever mindfulness means to you are great ways to honor your own health during your recovery period. Self-care is not just about being healthy but also about processing the loss. This could include exercise, yoga, stretching, massages, therapy, journaling, reading books on grief or healing, Facebook group chats, or evenings out with friends. Whatever resonates with you, go with that. Just make sure you address your own self-care head-on with some of these activities, and try not to ignore yourself and your needs any longer.

Nights were very difficult for me, and I found it hard to sleep, especially in the days following Samson's death. Sleep is critical for our healing, so aim for eight hours a night if you can. You might try supplements from a company like Equilibria if you need help with regular sleep in the aftermath of your loss (their CBD gummies for sleep are one of their best sellers).

Acknowledge that you won't be "normal" for a while. You will seem far away. You will forget things. You may be a zombie. It's okay, and it will pass. People will understand, and you should give yourself grace during this time. If you ever feel like you're losing it, try some breathing exercises. Put one hand on your heart and one on your belly. Breathe in for four seconds. Hold for four seconds. Breathe out for four seconds. Hold for four seconds. Repeat until you feel better.

Honor Your Pet's Legacy

Look at photos and videos of the good times. Smile as you relive the sweet memories. Laugh, cry, and talk to other people about your beloved pet. I think it's important to recognize and respect the negative parts of the experience (i.e., feelings of guilt, replaying what you wish you'd done differently), but we should also consciously revisit and honor the positive moments and memories. This is what our pets would want us to do, and it's what they think about when they remember us.

> Hold on tight to the good memories. It's easy to get caught up in the last moments and the time leading up to their eventual passing if it's expected. Take pictures, make a ceramic piece with their paw print. Just whatever you do, hold on to the good memories.
> —*Survey respondent*

You also might wish to formally remember or honor your pet. You might plan a memorial service, get a tattoo, order a custom necklace, or create a remembrance spot in your house or garden.

There is no one right answer, so you have to lean into what feels right. Will it make you happy to see your pet's remembrance spot every day? If so, you might display a picture of them, or their urn, pawprint, collar, favorite toy, or some other special items on a shelf or table near one of their go-to places in the house. If they loved to be outside, you might have a stone engraved with their name and/or headshot that can be placed in the yard where they often hung out.

One of the things I always gifted my sister when one of her pets passed away was a gift certificate to Etsy so she could buy a keepsake to remember her pet by. There are so many options: jewelry made of their ashes or fur, wind chimes, memorial boxes, and the list goes on.

While I'm not a tattoo person, it seems somewhat common for tattoo people to memorialize a soul companion in ink.

> I got a tattoo portrait of my dog on my arm. It really helps because people ask me about it and her a lot!
>
> —*Survey respondent*

Finally, a memorial service is something to consider, and it can be done at any point in time after their passing. I am planning to do one for Samson, but the timing hasn't felt right yet. Here's an example of the type of memorial service you might try:

1. Select a location that was meaningful to your pet (near the chair they often slept in, under their favorite tree in the garden, at a local park they loved, etc.)
2. Place a candle and a bowl of small objects on a table or the ground. I would select a white or pastel-colored candle, but anything other than black works. The small objects might be crystals, coins, bracelets, mini photo frames with a picture of your pet in it, or anything else that feels right. I'd include one item per person attending the service.
3. Ask everyone you've invited to sit or stand in a circle around the candle and bowl so all can see and hear.
4. Invite your pet to join in spirit if that feels right to you.
5. Begin the service by lighting the candle for your pet.
6. Read your pet's story aloud, or you could read a prayer or poem that resonates with you. You can see Samson's story as an example in the appendix, and I've also included the Rainbow Bridge poem on this book's website (https://www.petlossgrief.info), in case you'd like to read that. If you prefer to tell their story from memory, that works too.
7. Invite anyone present to share their favorite memory of your pet and any words they'd like to say as they honor your pet's life.
8. Impress positive healing energy onto the objects in the bowl. You

could do this by lighting a sage stick or paleo santo and waving it back and forth directly above the items while setting the intention of purification, positivity, and healing for all involved. You might sprinkle some water on the items. You could ask for a moment of silence while all participants send positive energy to the candle and the items in the bowl.

9. You can close by thanking everyone (and your pet) for coming. Give one of the small objects to each participant to keep and remember your pet by. Place your item on your pet's memorial shelf or display.

If the above seems too formal, you could also put together a picture and video slideshow, host a backyard barbeque or Zoom party, and go through the slideshow while celebrating your pet's life with festive food and drink.

Look for Signs from Your Pet

We've already talked about how to send loving energy to your pet with a Care Bear-style stare. Assuming you still feel connected to your pet, it's very likely you will experience magical moments after they pass.

Samson has sent me lots of yellow Labs and Golden Retrievers, several birds in unusual places, and my green necklace falling out of my purse when I needed a pick-me-up. I heard a puppy running through the halls in the weeks after his death. I believe he handpicked a dog for us to foster and adopt in order to expedite my healing—you'll read more about this in the last chapter. I also had a vision of spirits that inhabit the land near our Tennessee cabin, and I was comforted to see an outline of what looked like Samson's shadow on a wall during said vision.

Some people can feel their pet brush up against their leg, or they might see an unexplainable indentation on the sofa blankets where they used to sleep. In one of the pet-loss support groups on Facebook, I saw a very cool photograph taken with a nanny cam of a spirit dog curled up at the foot of his little girl's bed.

Signs and messages from your pet can take on many different shapes and colors. The important thing to remember if you hope to experience some of these things is to keep an open mind, because the animals really can work in mysterious ways.

Spend Time with Animals

If you have more pets at home, it's a good time to pour your heart into them. The siblings of passed pets can mourn and grieve their loss, so keeping up with normal routines is important for their healing. If you notice them exhibiting loss of appetite, lethargy, or aggression, you may need to consult a vet or trainer for assistance.

Some people are ready to adopt or get a new pet right away, while others don't think they will ever be ready.

> Losing such a big part of my life hurts, and I feel guilty loving another dog.
>
> —*Survey respondent*

I can say with confidence that your passed pet will be very happy if you decide to get another pet. They want you to love another pet, if that's something you want as well.

If you're not quite ready for a new dog or cat or you're like my friend

SAMSON'S STORY

Peggy and it was your one-and-done soul dog, you might volunteer at a local shelter or foster pets through a rescue organization. Other ideas include pet-sitting via Rover or hanging out with friends' pets for a few hours here and there.

Regardless of the manner in which you incorporate animals into your life right now, their power to heal is undeniable.

Get Through the Administrative Stuff

Sadly, there are some administrative items to handle when a pet passes away. You'll want to contact your vet(s), Chewy or other retailers who send you emails and mailers with your pet's name, your pet's daycare or boarding facility, and your pet's insurance company to alert them that your dog or cat has passed away. This step is terrible, but it's best to get through all of it in one sitting so you won't get random emails reminding you it's time for your passed pet's next annual checkup. I was pretty frustrated that Samson's Chicago vet had to be told twice that he had passed away. I understand they see lots of pets and may not remember each one, but I also believe that it's important to not screw up on such a life-changing thing.

At some point, you'll also want to address their belongings in the house. What will you do with any items that didn't make the memorial shelf? When you consider their leash, bed, blankets, medicines, food and water bowls, and toys, what will you throw away, donate, or save for a future pet?

> One of the hardest things is cleaning up and getting rid of Zeus's things, because it makes it seem or look like he was never there. That hurts because he was, and he matters, and I don't want him forgotten.

—Survey respondent

The Grief Recovery Handbook for Pet Loss has a great approach for figuring out what to do with your pet's items. They call it the ABC plan. In summary, you put all of your pet's belongings in one place and go through them one at a time. You decide where each one goes:

- Pile A: things you definitely want to keep
- Pile B: things you definitely want to throw away, give away, or donate
- Pile C: anything you're not yet sure about

You can go ahead and place the Pile A items wherever you want to keep them long term. The Pile B items can be processed immediately, so throw away what you need to, and give away or donate the usable items. Place the Pile C belongings in a box in the garage for a month. Then, pull it out and divide the items into Piles A, B, and C again. You might have to do it once more a few months later to make all the decisions. Waiting a month or two on any undecided items is really smart. I have a friend who got rid of all of her dog's toys right after he died and is now sad that she did.

Ignore These Things if You Hear Them

I was pretty shocked by some of the things I heard from other people who learned of Samson's illness or passing. I took it all in stride, but I wish I could educate the general public to never say these things to someone who has lost a pet:

- At least they lived a good long life.
- At least they're not in pain or suffering any longer.
- You did the right thing.

- It's a good thing you have other fur babies to love.
- When will you adopt your next pet?
- You can always get another one.
- They were just a dog or cat, thankfully.
- I know how much you loved your pet.
- I know how you feel.

I heard a lot of the first two, which was frustrating. I heard a little of the "you did the right thing," which I also didn't love. There was even a dog mom in the park who told me while he was still alive that Samson looked tired and was ready to go. I could have punched her in the face. I still avoid her in the park to this day as I have zero respect for her. I personally wasn't as upset by comments such as "I know how much you loved your pet," and "I know how you feel," but I acknowledge these statements could be upsetting to some.

Instead, the only things people should say to you are, "I'm sorry to hear of your pet's passing," and "I'm here for you." They get bonus points if they say and truly mean, "If I can do anything to help or if you just want to talk, let me know."

Please refer your friends and family to this page or Appendix 5 for more information on how to talk to people going through pet loss. I'd also remind people to check in multiple times when someone has lost a pet, not just once. There were a few people who did that with me, and I really appreciated it.

One other thing I wish I could change is the propensity people have to send flowers post-death. Or at least get people to ask if the grieving pet parents want flowers. I personally hated getting flowers only to watch them die. One of our neighbors gifted us a perennial to plant in Samson's honor. I loved that idea because it would grow back each season, and we could plant it near where he liked to lie in the grass at our cabin. Other safe but meaningful ideas include sending gift certificates for food, house cleaning, or an Etsy gift.

Chapter 8

LETTERS TO SAMSON

After writing Samson's story, I felt like it was important to share how I processed things the three months after his death. I wasn't sure how to address this part of the book, so I asked for Samson's help one night. I clearly heard "write me letters." So that's what I did. Not every day, but whenever I felt like I had something important to share with Samson that might also resonate with readers going through the same rebuilding process. And as I was re-reading my animal communication notes, I realized he said the same thing to Jaime Breeze: write him letters. ☺

May 18th

Dear Samson, I am so sad you left us today, and I haven't wrapped my head around it yet. The immediate emotion is relief, and there's such a lightness in the house now that you aren't suffering. Thank you for sending us signs right away. The flock of birds' synchronicity gave us comfort, as did seeing a duck in the street—your first "bird in an unusual place."

Despite the relief, I also feel numb. I have to do things to keep my mind off the heaviness of losing you. You were such an important part of our lives, and we are lost without you. I can tell Murphy is just as upset as your Dad and I are.

This terrible day ended in a bittersweet moment when Mrs. Amy came over unexpectedly, and we learned you were honored at the Live Like Roo party tonight. I wished with all my heart you had made it there, as I know you loved a good party. But thank you for coming to me at the fire and letting me know you had already crossed off your whole bucket list. I'm so glad you feel you lived your life to the fullest.

May 19th

Dear Samson, My first morning without you. It is quite gut wrenching when I think of you so often and how I need to check on you or I'll get to see you in a bit. And it's all a fleeting notion. Because you're gone. At least your body is. I know you're still here in spirit, but it's just not the same because I can't hug your sweet neck anymore. I can't sing you good morning songs and feed you and let you outside.

Luckily, we had the neighborhood yard sale today. We gave away your extra Milk-Bones to dogs that walked by, as I know you'd not want them to go to waste. So many neighbors gave us hugs as they passed by and were sorry to hear of our loss. They knew what a big soul and presence you were, and they all loved you too. The little girl who laid by you at your party in the park brought me a wildflower. Ace—the puppy who loved saying hi to you almost every day for the past week—and his mom stopped by. She asked where you were, and

I had to tell her we said goodbye to you yesterday. She had no idea you were even sick, and despite my sea of pain, that made my heart so happy.

May 21st

My dearest boy, It's weird without you here in the house. Nighttime is so hard for me. I am mostly okay during the day as long as I stay busy, but nights allow the panic to roll in like a bad storm. It's the hardest thing in the world thinking about your body lying somewhere right now waiting for cremation. Murphy is also really struggling—he tried to bite someone at daycare today which he's never done before, and he isn't eating normally.

We decided to escape to Tennessee for a week to see if it's any easier there. When we left the cabin, we didn't know you were sick, so we hope it doesn't remind us of the last few weeks like our Chicago house does.

The road trip started out pretty rocky, as Murphy was very anxious. He was inconsolable and just plain awful during the first sixty minutes of our drive. It was like a kick in the pants to have to acknowledge that our well-adjusted, sweet, easy-to-parent dog is now gone. I would be lying if I didn't admit wanting to trade Murphy for you today. I feel bad about that now, but in the moment, I would have done it in a heartbeat.

In happier news, you'd be pleased to know that Murphy will get to ride on The Magic Dog Bus one day this week!

May 22nd

Dear Samson, I finally had the courage to send the sad news today to Dr. Roni, your favorite vet.

Hi Dr. Roni,

I am so sad to share with you that we lost our boy on Saturday. He wasn't doing great during the day on Friday, and we made an at-home appointment to say goodbye on Monday morning. When we went to give him some medicine on Friday night, he was shaking pretty badly, and Matt and I realized he may not make it to Monday—so we changed the appointment to Saturday at noon. We slept outside with him on Friday night and gave him one more car ride on Saturday morning—he sure loved being outside & taking car rides. It was as peaceful as I could have hoped. I cannot believe our Samson is gone now and so quickly too—he was such a special boy and will be missed by so many.

I brought a plant in today to thank you and your team for caring for him—Samson wrote a note on the bottom. He really loved to go and see you all, and our family thanks you so much for your kindness and help with his mobility treatments and also with advice over the past few weeks.

I wish I had more time with him, but I think this is what he chose. I was hoping he would get at least one good season with us here in TN, and he literally waited until the day we got back to Chicago to let us know he was sick—so mommy got her one good season with her boy. For his last 2.5 weeks, he was able to lay out in the front yard and see lots of people and dogs—another one of his favorite things!

SAMSON'S STORY

I'm actually bringing Murphy in for an appt. at your hospital tomorrow at 230. He's displayed some behavior issues at daycare since Samson's passing, and we are going to ask about anxiety medicine. I feel for the little guy—I believe he is as devastated as I am about losing his best friend.

Thank you again,
Gale (and Samson)

Dear Gale,

We are so very sorry for your loss. There are really no words that can do justice to the loss we feel when one of our treasured canine soul mates passes. All you can do is make that part of our shared journey with them as peaceful and caring as possible. Minimize the anxiety, stress and pain, and reassure that love is the standard and foundation of that relationship. You have done this completely and with grace and consideration for Samson. Well done. I so very much wanted him to have a little more time, but we all did what we could to make what we had pretty darn good. Thank you for allowing us to be part of Samson's journey. You all have been a pleasure to work with. Samson was the perfect rehab patient....the kind we look forward to helping. He made us laugh and helped make us feel like we were accomplishing something. Thank you for making us part of his team.
Dr. Roni

May 23rd

I booked Murphy on The Magic Dog Bus today as I think it will really cheer him up to see Mrs. Amy and Mrs. Jennifer, the bus driver, and his bus friends. I feel so empty after opening the app to request the appointment. Your profile picture was there next to Murphy's, and it said "deceased" across it. Talk about crying ugly tears. I immediately texted Amy a screenshot, and she was appalled and promised to reach out to Run Loyal, the app maker. The engineers are obviously not pet parents, as no pet parent in their right mind would ever want to see that.

May 25th

Dear Sammie, It's still hard in Tennessee even though you didn't have your sunset season here. Everything is a reminder of you. I want to focus on the good and honor your memory and legacy. But it's also so unbearable to know I'll never see my lion walking out in the pasture again. My how I loved to stand on the back deck and watch you walk around, sniffing to your heart's content. Everything still feels surreal, as it's just been five days since we bid you farewell. Even the rugs make me sad. I have to decide what I'm going to do with the runners I bought to make it easier for you to walk around here. I knew in the back of my mind there would be a day when I wouldn't need a dozen rugs strewn about to help you get a better grip on the floor. That day is here, and I'm heartbroken.

May 28th

Dear Samson, We drove back to Chicago today. There's a huge empty space in our car now without you, but we were able to transport a Boston terrier from Nashville. His adopters met us at our house when we arrived—it felt good to help. This is one small way we can honor your legacy—I know you would have loved this sweet little Boston terrier pup.

SAMSON'S STORY

May 29th

Dearest Samson, Your dad and I picked up your remains today. That was one of the hardest things for me so far. I could barely talk as we drove the ten minutes to their location. I rang the bell, and a gal met us outside with a navy-blue bag. Your urn and ashes, pawprint, nose print, and lock of fur were in the bag. I held your ashes in my lap and wailed in the car for several blocks. I wish more than ever I could see you again. I'm glad your body isn't lying in a freezer somewhere any longer and it's back home. What I wouldn't give to see you just one more time.

May 30th

Sammie, I took my first flight today after losing you. I cried as we took off because I knew you weren't going to be there when I came home. That was always my favorite thing about traveling—that I'd get to come home to you and your brother. I felt your presence on the plane today, and I talked to you about this being your first trip with Mommy and you'd get to see what it's like when Mommy leaves for a long run. You were excited to be with me! I know I'm still so sad, but thank you for being here with me in spirit.

June 5th

Dear Samson, Your dad is gone on a business trip, and I've heard a puppy run down the hall three times in the past two days. It's you, isn't it? I'm so glad you'll be coming back to us as a puppy in the future. It won't be the exact same, but I'll know it's your soul when I meet you again.

June 8th

Hi Samson, I was a bit sad tonight while getting ready to go out with friends. Just before we left the house, my emerald necklace fell out of a purse I haven't used in a few months. I'd actually forgotten it was there—don't tell your dad! As soon as it fell into my hand, I smiled. A green surprise. I knew it was another sign from you, just like you told me.

I've been wearing the Samson necklace Aunt Peggy gave me four years ago. I didn't wear it nearly enough when you were alive, but I wear it every day now. I'm going to start wearing the emerald necklace and the Samson necklace together, as they both remind me of you.

June 10th

Dear Samson, I saw Aunt Chiara today in San Francisco. I was telling her your story and how you told me you'd send retrievers, birds in unusual places, and green and pink things my way as a sign you were around. Just as I told her that, I noticed the ice cube in the Aperol Spritz I was drinking had a duck etched in it. Definitely an usual place for a bird. I'm grateful for these signs, my boy!

A duck ice cube—sign from Samson?

SAMSON'S STORY

June 14th

Dear Sam, It was Daddy's 40th birthday today. I reread the card you wrote to him just before you died, and I cried so much. We miss you every day. We think of you every day. I still feel like I'm going through the motions. Just trying to put one foot in front of the other. Go to work, put activities on the calendar, work on this book. Anything that will make time move forward. Even though I don't want to live like everything is normal, I know it's part of the process to reintegrate into life. I'm so grateful you continue to send me signs. Today, at the Cubs game, we heard the men behind us quoting Samsonite a few times (from the movie Dumb and Dumber). It made me smile. I look forward to the time where there are more smiles than the feeling of complete heartbreak that still creeps across my entire body at least once a day.

June 15th

Dear Samson, We donated some of your items to the Chicagoland Lab Rescue today. I know you would want other pups to be able to use your extra medicine, treats, and supplements. We also told Kim who runs the rescue to keep us in mind for a foster dog soon. Either a mellow senior yellow Lab or a puppy—we think your brother Murphy has the highest chance of success in those two cases. I know we aren't ready to adopt a new dog yet, but I think it will be helpful for your brother to have other dogs around right now. He's really struggling without you—we always said you were his favorite person. ☺

June 16th

Dear Sam, I cut up an apple this evening and grabbed a spoonful of peanut butter. Murphy came up to me as he smelled the peanut butter, looking for his treat. It's been nearly a month since you've passed away, and it hit me hard—this is the first time Murph is doing what was so normal for him to do. Each day you'd take morning and evening pills with peanut butter, and Murph was right there to get a lick from the spoon when you were done. I gave Murph a small spoonful of peanut butter tonight, and I ugly cried as he licked it up. You should be here. Nothing is the same.

June 17th

Dear Samson, I notice everything that reminds me of my past. I pass a restaurant where I met Aunt Bailey in 2014, and I tell myself I would go back to that time in an instant because you and I would have our whole experience yet to come. I pass a park you and I visited back in late 2017, and I want to teleport back to that day and time. I suppose this is my version of bargaining during the grief process. Even just eating pasta made with sauce we bought at a store the last day before we drove back from TN makes me sad. I can't eat it without thinking how I bought this before I knew you were sick. I pick out something to wear—I grab shorts, and my mind immediately assesses that I haven't worn them since you were by my side, alive and well. Everything seems to be categorized into three time periods—before you were sick, when you were still here but sick, and the current time period when you're gone.

June 18th

Dear Sammie, It's been exactly one month since we said goodbye to you. I think Murphy is finally getting better and not as depressed, but I do not feel like I've personally made much progress to be honest. For example, today was the first time I went to a store with Daddy and Murphy waiting in the car. I came out and couldn't talk as I realized my big yellow boy wasn't there to greet me. These firsts where you aren't here are glaringly obvious and heartbreaking. I try to still talk to you during the day, but it's not the same.

June 19th

Dearest Samson, Grief is an interesting thing. For me, staying busy is helpful. But I can't work all the time, and we already finished watching Bridgerton. I sometimes watch random documentaries or old movies I know will be mindless. Today, I selected *Practical Magic* because I'd seen a Facebook post talking about how Nicole Kidman and Sandra Bullock were signed on to film a sequel. I had to rewind twice to make sure I heard it right, but the horse's name in the movie is Samson. It does offer some kind of peace to get these signs. Thank you for sending them, my sweet boy.

June 22nd

Dear Samson, I know I'm not supposed to feel guilt. I know I did everything right based on what I knew at the time. And I did it out of love. But I feel the guilt. Why didn't I notice your elevated liver and kidney enzyme levels? They were still in the "normal" range so the vet didn't flag it, but I should have seen it. I'm your Mommy. I knew something was wrong with you in December—we tested for Cushing's, Addison's, Leptospirosis, and a urinary tract infection and couldn't find anything. I should have kept looking for answers. Your eating habits changed quite a bit in your final months, and I didn't dig into the why. I know you told the animal communicators you likely would have passed years earlier if I wasn't your Mommy, but I know in my heart you had a year or two left. I feel like I failed you.

June 24th

Dear Sam, I believe there is a bigger purpose to all of this. I know I'll do something with my animal communication gifts. It's likely something revolving around pet health/longevity and maybe pet grief. I came home from my third trip since you've been gone. It's no easier than the first one. The house is empty without you, even though I do believe your spirit is still here. I've read that spirits stick around for a few months, and I will be sad when we get to the point where you might not be here as often.

June 28th

Dear Samson, Hearing the "beep beep beep" of the trash truck was hard this morning. I couldn't even bring myself to go outside and see Mr. Bobby—you should be here to run down your ramp and anxiously wait for Milk-Bones to fall from the sky. I found your collar today when I was picking up before Mrs. Tracy came to clean. I held it in my hands and wept. I still feel your presence everywhere. But you should be here in your fluffy yellow body. It's just not right without you here. Murphy laid by me on the chaise part of the couch, and I moved him around and said "there it goes" out of habit. That's what I used to say to you when I'd readjust your body as you lay next to me. I hadn't said it in well over a month, and it was so familiar yet so foreign as it rolled off my tongue.

July 3rd

Hi Sammie, I got my first Apple watch today, and I love the feature where I can see a different picture of you whenever I check the time. It was painful to set up the "Samson" album initially, but I enjoy seeing the old memories come up. They make me smile. I also included some of the photos from your sunset season; I'm glad I have those too because they're part of our story. But it's time for Mommy to really lean into the love and good memories. There's nothing I can do to bring you back my sweet boy. I dearly wish that were the case. Losing you has been the hardest thing I've gone through in my life. I've been reading a book called *Journey of Souls* which has really helped me understand where your soul is right now when you're between lives on Earth. I realize you and I likely have had many lives together, and that's why I feel so close to you. This is the exact reason people use the term soul dog or heart dog. And Samson, you are definitely one of my soul dogs, and likely my brightest soul dog if I had to guess.

July 5th

Dear Samson, A few weeks ago, I joined some Facebook groups for dogs with mobility issues to see if I could find somewhere to donate your wheelchair. I randomly was served up a group called "Librela—the Truth." I thought, "Interesting, Samson had a Librela shot in November 2023" and joined it. I've now read quite a lot of posts in this group; many dog parents have given their pups the Librela shot and then regretted it deeply as they ultimately believe the shot contributed to their dog's death. Today, I read a number of cases that were quite similar to yours, and I realize my sweet boy, that the shot I let the vet give you on Nov. 10th last year may very well have led to complications that took you from us too soon. I knew something was wrong with you in December, and we did all those tests. We couldn't figure it out, but your side effects are a near one-to-one match for many of these other cases involving Librela. I'm heartbroken I didn't know to detox you from this drug. I'm so sorry I let the vet give you the shot. Now I know why you likely couldn't stand at all for a short spell and why your kidneys and liver may have failed. I've seen videos of other dogs who can't lift their hind end just like you couldn't when we ordered you that wheelchair.

It's so sad that a pharmaceutical company is giving this medicine to dogs and cats when there have been thousands of adverse reaction reports, and the pet parents in this facebook group are devasted. They wish they'd known the side effects. They wish they'd known that former cancer patients and those with kidney, neurological, or cognitive issues should never be given the drug. I am gutted that we didn't know this, as you did have cancer a few years before and also neurological issues. When the vet told us it's a miracle drug with no side effects, well that just wasn't true.

[On December 16, 2024, the FDA published a letter to veterinarians detailing the results of their analysis of adverse events reported in dogs who had been treated with Librela; the administration recommended adding a number of potential side effects to the label, including death. For more information on Samson's case study regarding Librela, please see Appendix 3.]

July 7th

Dear Samson, A few weeks ago, I reached out to the gals from the Chicagoland Lab Rescue where we adopted you. I told them we wanted to foster a bunch of dogs this summer, largely to help Murphy acclimate to having dogs in the house now that you're gone. Truth be told, I knew I needed another dog around too as the grief has been so hard for me. Today, we were supposed to pick up our first foster named Lilly. She looks almost exactly like you, Samson! Sadly, we didn't get to meet her as the overnight foster family loved her so much, they kept her. Based on how sweet she looked and if she was anything like you, I'm not at all surprised they kept her!

July 10th

Dear Samson, It was an especially hard day for me, as the grief was heavy. I just feel super sad all the time now. I'm so thankful you came to me as I lay awake in bed tonight, when I was feeling really sad. It was the first true "download" style communication I've experienced, and I'm honored it came from you. You gave me a lot of advice about how to move forward, how to help other pet parents with their grief, and how I should address Zoetis, the maker of Librela, with "love words" not "hate words." That is so like you to say. The most surprising message was that we'd be getting a third dog! Finally, I'm glad cousin Cooper was with you, and I hope you two are having fun together on the other side!

July 11th

Dear Sam, Today was the second annual Women's Entrepreneurship Event I host in Chicago. It went really well. Lots of great speakers, and I invite men to join because everyone should be part of the conversation when it comes to supporting women in starting businesses. Yet the event was bittersweet for me. You see, last year, the reason I sent you to daycare for a day was the first annual event on November 9, 2023. And when I picked you up from daycare that evening, you were struggling to walk. I had dropped off a totally normal dog, and I think the slick floors at daycare did a number on you, my sweet boy. The next day, I took you to the vet to make sure you were okay. That's the day they gave you the Librela shot. I hate that day. So I hate the women's event a little bit. I know you wouldn't want me to hate it because it's doing good in the world. But I can't help it. I wish I could go back to that day in November last year and do it differently. I'd have paid someone to come to our house and stay with you during the event. Then, you wouldn't have been limping, and you'd never have gotten the shot. And you might still be here with me today.

July 13th

Dear Samson, Today, Honey Snow, a beautiful white Lab and Pyrenees mix puppy was going to be our first foster dog. But we got the text again that the family keeping her overnight decided to adopt her. So no dog for us would be on the transport from southern Missouri. I cried desperate tears when I got the news. I really needed Honey Snow as I think helping other dogs will allow me to begin healing the deep wound your passing has left on my heart. Please help us get a foster dog soon!

July 16th

Dear Samson, Your Dad is traveling again, and I'm trying to clean up the basement a bit. Your wheelchair has been sitting there since you passed, and I know I have to donate it. So today is the day. I parked behind the Wild Hearts facility just a few miles from where we live and rang the bell. I held my breath, willing myself not to cry. A nice woman came to the door. I told her I was there to donate your wheelchair (I'd already called in advance so she knew I was coming). I told her a bit about your story and asked about the dogs Wild Hearts works with. They are mostly senior dogs with mobility issues. Your kindred spirits. I asked her if any had come through with mobility issues potentially caused by Librela. She said yes, a handful had. So very sad. I said goodbye and turned to leave, feeling the tears threaten to pour out. She thanked me for the donation and said she was sorry for my loss. "Thank you," I said, turning to get into the car, and then the tears came. Saying thank you to that sentiment is just weird. But what do you say when you've lost your soul dog? There is nothing to say. There are just the good memories, and there are of course the throat lumps and tears that still show up often nearly two months after I said goodbye to you.

July 18th

It's been exactly two months since you left your physical body behind. We got new gutters today—I guess one of the silver linings of not having you to take care of is having time to cross some house to-dos off our list. Dad's been traveling but came home tonight. I bought wood, and we made a fire. We haven't had a lot of fires since you passed away. It was something we did when you were around. But today on the two-month anniversary, it felt fitting.

July 20th

Dear Samson, Our first foster actually showed up on the transport! I picked up Callie from Tinley Park this morning. The last dogs we fostered through the Chicagoland Lab Rescue were Duke and Ellie, and before that, Dolly. All great dogs. And Callie is no different. Such a sweetie. I've posted about her in the Facebook neighborhood group and hope someone nearby will adopt her. It's nice to have a second dog in the house again, and Murphy loves his new friend. It was a bit difficult for him at first, because you know how he likes to protect his house and pack. But once he realized she would play with him anytime he wants, he was very happy. No one will ever fill your paws, Samson, but it does ease my heartache a bit to have another pup around. It helps that she's cuddly and will lie by me like you used to. I think fostering was the right call because we can make sure we are 100% ready before we adopt another dog.

Foster puppy Callie.

July 25th

Dear Sam, Callie was adopted today! And I'm in Tennessee riding on The Magic Dog Bus to a pitch event. Mrs. Amy did an amazing job and won second place and $3,000. It was so nice to see all of the gals from the dog bus, but it was especially comforting to know that you got to ride the bus twice and absolutely loved it. I cherish those memories of you having so much fun on The Magic Dog Bus and getting a pup cup from the local coffee shop!

July 27th

Dear Samson, Dad picked me up from the airport, and we went straight to get our new foster, Lark, from Bolingbrook. Lark is a very cute yellow Lab or Golden Retriever mix. She's only four to five months old and weighs almost 40 pounds already! She's very sweet and cuddly and kind of reminds us of you a bit. Murphy welcomed her quickly and has been playing with her non-stop, so he definitely approves of his new foster sister.

SAMSON'S STORY

Lark, our next foster pup.

July 29th

Dear Samson, Aunt Laura came over to meet Lark, and she immediately asked where you were. I moved your ashes, collar, wooden plaque with your handsome face on it, pawprint, and fur clipping from the mantel to a more permanent spot on the bottom shelf of the enclosed glass cabinet in the living room. Your ashes and personal things are right by one of the dog beds so you can hang out by the pups who lie there. It was one of your favorite places in our house during your last few weeks with us. Also, Aunt Laura thinks I should adopt Lark. So does our neighbor Mrs. Grace. So does everyone we meet in the park. Lark does have your energy, Samson. She is very sweet and gentle and walks up to everyone she meets for pets and treats, just like you did.

August 3rd

Dear Sammie, I'm in Lewes, Delaware today visiting Aunt Tracy and Uncle Ed and some of my other friends from college. You came with us twice to Lewes on two different road trips. I am sitting on the same couch you liked to sit on just like a person—upright with a strong lean into the back of the couch. It is comforting to know you were here. I wish I'd taken more photos. I only have eight photos from our 2019 trip and just four from 2020. In the 2019 ones, you're wading through the water at Rehoboth Beach, and you're loving life. Last night, we walked right by where you and I were once together at that very beach, and I couldn't stop thinking about you. And one of the pictures from our 2020 trip is you lying on the carpet in their house. I asked Ed where in the house it was, and he said you were lying behind Aunt Tracy's desk. When I got back from the beach today, I went and sat in that very spot and cried. I can feel your presence here with me. You loved the adventures. You loved the beach, even in winter. Maybe especially in winter. You loved to see your friends—dogs and people both. My heart is full from your love, but man I miss you buddy.

August 5th

Dear Samson, I've been trying to decide what to do with Lark. Should we adopt her? We weren't planning to adopt a dog here in Chicago as there is such a huge need in Tennessee. But she's stolen our hearts. I've gone back and forth all day, and this evening it popped into my head what day it was. It's your Gotcha Day, Samson. I adopted you on August 5, 2017. And in that moment, I knew. She's technically the third foster since your July 10th visit in spirit because Honey Snow would have been number one if she hadn't been adopted. Plus you told me you'd send me birds in unusual ways, and isn't it curious that she's named after a bird? But it also overlaps perfectly with your adoption day. So we listened to these signs from you. Tonight, we decided to adopt Lark on August 5, 2024, exactly seven years after you made me a dog mom. Her official name will be Meadowlark Samson Wilkinson—Lark for short.

SAMSON'S STORY

August 6th

Dear Sam, I went to the Cubs game with Aunt Bailey today. Daddy dropped me off in your car. Little Lark was in the back seat, and boy does she look like you when she rides in the car with us. She loves rides just like you did, without a care as to where we're going so long as she's with us. Sometimes she sits up and leans back into the seat like you used to, and she also likes to put her head right by the open window to get the good breezes. Your favorite. When Daddy pulled away, Lark's little yellow head with ears perked up looked so much like you that I had to take a picture. I miss you so much, but it's a little bit easier when this kind, gentle soul you sent us reminds us of some of the sweet things you used to do.

Lark looking out the window in the back seat, just like Samson used to do.

August 9th

Dear Samson, Early this morning, we heard the "beep beep beep." Friday trash service was very early today! Murphy was still home as we hadn't even gotten up yet, so this was probably the first time he'd heard the truck backing down our alley since the day before you died. Murph started pacing by the bedroom door, and I realized he might remember that the beeping equals dog treats in the yard. Even though Mr. Bobby retired six weeks ago, and his replacement does not give out Milk-Bones, I let Murph out into the yard to see what he'd do. Yep, his ears perked up as he awaited the launch of the bones. Just like your ears used to perk up. Murph may have only been with you half a dozen times in the past 2.5 years for Friday bones, but he remembered. I sure wish you were here to saunter down your ramp and search for Milk-Bones in the yard with your brother and new sister.

August 10th

Dear Sam, I initially couldn't bring myself to wash the blanket you laid on during your last car ride. It's been folded in the closet since that terrible day. I've smelled it a few times over the past few months, hoping it would smell like you. It doesn't. It kind of has that musty generic dog smell, and it's been a comfort to know that you laid on it while you were still here. But today I decided it was time to wash it. I pulled it out and sat down on the floor with Lark. I let her smell it in case she might pick up your scent. I told her it was your blanket, and she would have loved you so much. And I cried. Sweet Lark sat by me and licked the tears off my face.

August 18th

Dear Samson, It's been three months without you today. Each monthly anniversary gets a tiny bit easier, but I still miss you so much. Yesterday was Mr. Bobby the garbage collector's retirement party. Matt and I took Lark. I always thought you'd be around to celebrate his retirement, and it kills me that you died just six weeks shy of his last trash run. He loved all the dogs on his route, but he admitted to us yesterday that you were his favorite, my sweet boy.

SAMSON'S STORY

August 27th

I got a text message today from Wild Hearts. It was a message I'd requested and hoped for, but honestly I forgot about until it came through. Wild Hearts sent pictures and videos of a senior jet black shepherd girl named Raisen learning to use your wheelchair. They said, "Hello Gale. Raisen wanted to thank you and Samson for her new wheels. She's hoping to use the wheels to regain some strength and control in her hind limbs, and get back to walking on her own." I cried big tears and smiled as I watched the videos of her excelling in your chair and hearing the laughter of her trainer and parents. I know you'd be overjoyed to be helping another senior dog. You're a healer and a teacher. And your legacy lives on.

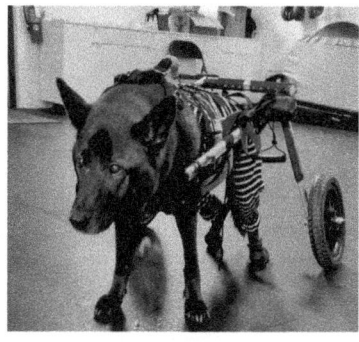

Raisen using the wheels Samson donated to Wild Hearts!

August 30th

My Dearest Samson, Daddy told Lark to "fill up the tank" today before we went outside for our morning walk. It was the first time I'd heard it since you passed away. We always used that phrase with you because you knew when it was time to go outside, and you'd go to the water bowl and drink, drink, drink so you'd have a full tank to mark your spots on our walk. We comment all the time how Lark is so similar to you in so many ways, but it still stops us in our tracks when we say or hear something that is 100% reminiscent of you. Lately, these things have started to make me smile more than cry. And I know I'm finally getting better. I will never heal completely my boy. But I've healed enough that I finally figured out today how to incorporate the grief and guilt sections into the book. I think I had to go through the majority of the process myself to be able to relay it to others. So this will be my last official letter to you, my Samson. I want to thank you one more time for all the unconditional love, smiles, puppy runs, head nudges, woo woos, and signs from beyond. I'm so grateful you sent Lark to us because without her, I don't think I would have gotten to this point. And now, I wait for you to come back as a new pup. Before you left, you told us how excited you were to fly. To go fast. To be free. I'm okay now my boy. So be free and fly fast. I will find you again, and I can't wait to hug your sweet soul once more.

[the end]

Appendix 1

ADDITIONAL READING

The Forever Dog by Rodney Habib and Dr. Karen Shawn Becker—this book is packed with information on pet nutrition and health that is helpful when your dog is in its sunset season. I wish I'd read it much earlier in Samson's life.

The Dog Cancer Survival Guide by Dremian Dressler and Dr. Susan Ettinger—a book you might want to read if your dog is affected by cancer. Warning: it's very long, so you might skim through to find the information that is most relevant to you!

The Grief Recovery Handbook for Pet Loss by Russell Friedman, Cole James, and John W. James—this book walks you through the process of creating a graphical timeline of the relationship you had with your pet and resolving any remaining issues by writing a grief recovery letter and holding a memorial service.

How to ROAR: Pet Loss Grief Recovery by Robin Jean Brown—A workbook that contains guided journal exercises to complete as you process your pet loss.

Good Grief: Finding Peace After Pet Loss by Sid Korpi—a compilation of short stories about real pet loss cases and how their parents dealt with the grief.

The Amazing Afterlife of Animals by Karen A. Anderson—this book shares many magical examples of how pets can send us messages after they pass away.

Journey of Souls by Michael Newton—a book that chronicles what happens to souls after death and before they enter their next life. While it discusses human souls, I believe the content is also relevant to animal souls.

Appendix 2

SURVEY DATA RESULTS

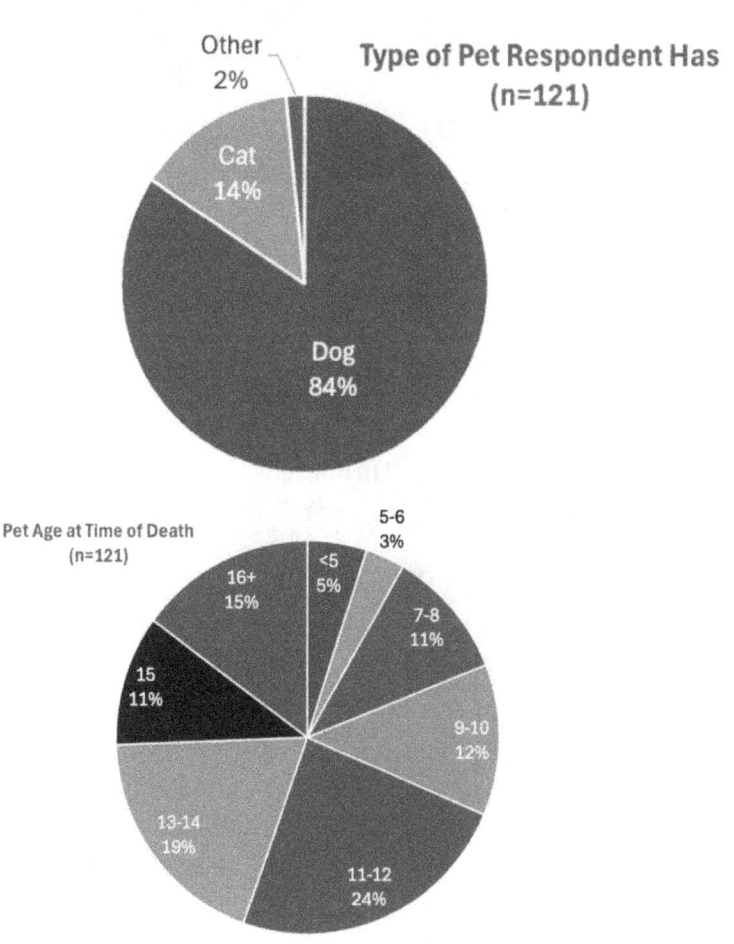

193

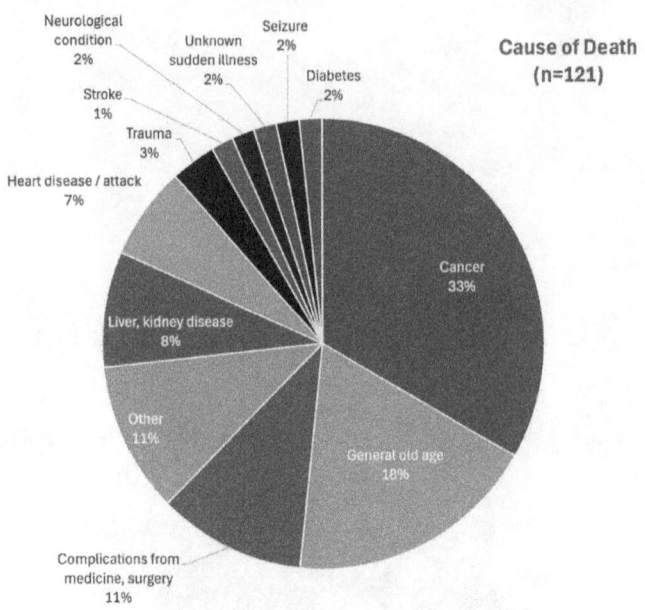

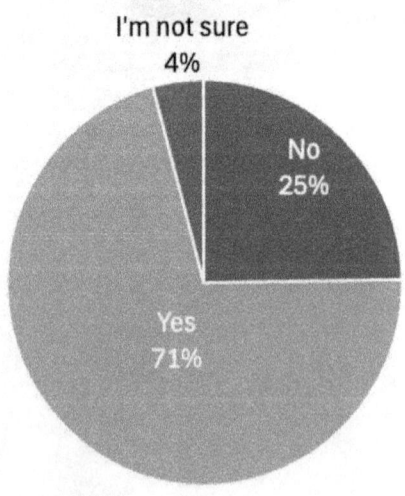

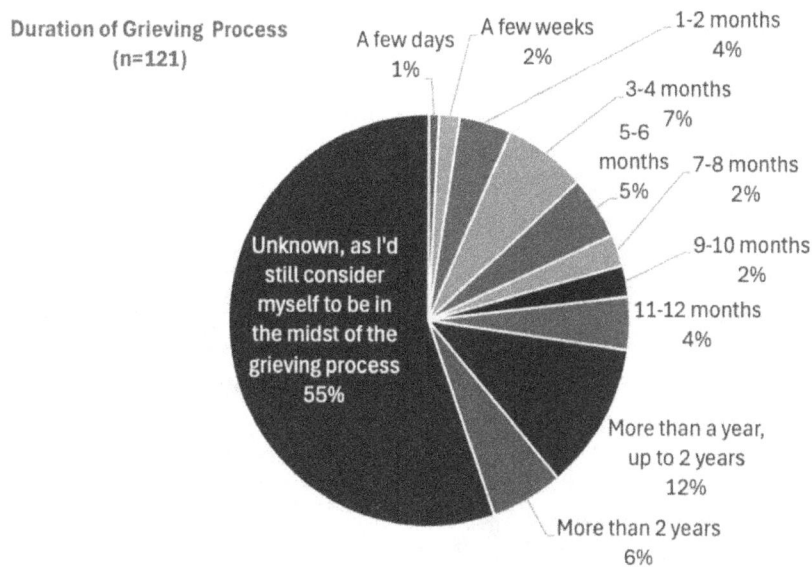

Note about the chart above: quite a few people who responded have recently lost a pet, so the Unknown percentage may be higher than it would be if we could control for the entire sample population losing a pet around the same time.

If we only look at the people who responded with an answer other than "unknown", the average duration of the grieving process is approximately 13 months (n=54).

Did a vet give an estimated amount of time your pet had left when you learned they were at the end of life? (n=121)

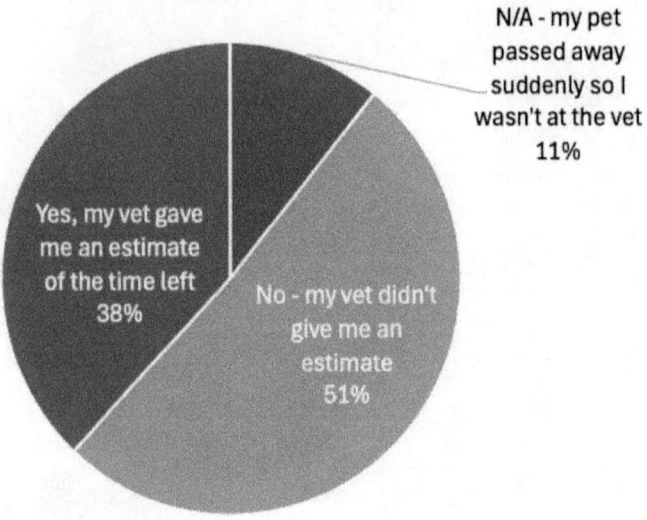

- Yes, my vet gave me an estimate of the time left: 38%
- No - my vet didn't give me an estimate: 51%
- N/A - my pet passed away suddenly so I wasn't at the vet: 11%

Actual Days Lived vs. Vet Estimate (n=47)

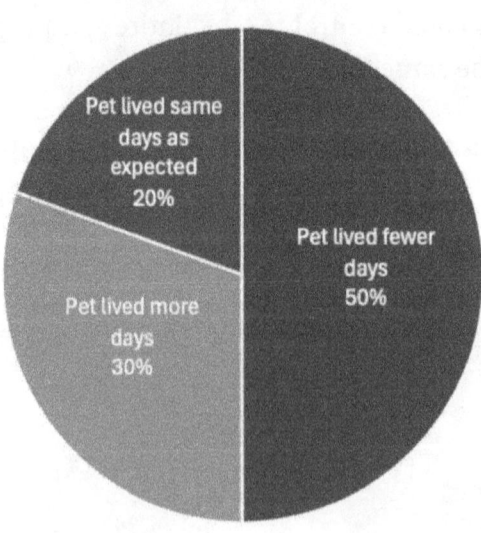

- Pet lived same days as expected: 20%
- Pet lived more days: 30%
- Pet lived fewer days: 50%

The final three questions are open-ended ones that I coded and compiled. Some respondents did not answer, and some respondents mentioned multiple things. This is why the percentages will not add up to 100. I divide the number of mentions by the total respondents (121).

If you feel any guilt about the death of your pet, could you please share what that guilt is about? (n=121)

<u>Caregiving role & decisions – 51%</u>
I generally let them down / couldn't protect or save them – 11%
I didn't notice signs; I wish I'd seen their illness earlier – 10%
I should have questioned the vet more / done more research – 9%
I couldn't afford the care – 6%
I wish I'd made different care decisions & the outcome could have been better – 5%
I got mad at them for having accidents in the house before I realized they were sick – 2%
Watching them suffer / wondering if they suffered – 2%
I didn't protect them from the accident – 2%
If we did something that caused the cancer (ie smoking around them) – 2%
Yelling at them – 1%
I wonder if I should have got them a friend & they would have lived longer – 1%
I always assumed they would be healthy – 1%
I'm not sure how they got sick – 1%
I didn't take them to the vet enough – 1%

<u>Euthanasia decisions – 21%</u>
I made the decision to put them down; I feel like I killed them – 7%
I wonder if I put them down too late – 7%

I wonder if I put them down too soon – 4%
Not knowing when to put them down – 2%
I didn't make the choice to euthanize and wish I had – 2%
I should have done something specific during the procedure and I regret it – 1%

<u>Quality time & being there for them – 15%</u>
I should have spent more time with them & done more of what they loved – 7%
I wasn't physically there at the end – 7%
I didn't take them home for a week of doing the things they loved before euthanasia – 1%
There wasn't time for my daughter to say goodbye – 1%

What helped you heal the most after the death of your pet? (n=121)

<u>Honoring my passed pet – 43%</u>
Remembering good memories through stories & looking at pictures / videos – 12%
Memorials (displayed ashes, made memory stones, painted their picture, tattoo, etc.) – 9%
Talking about my passed pet – 5%
Knowing they lived a wonderful and full life – 4%
Signs they are still here; feeling their presence; knowing they may reincarnate – 3%
Knowing they were the best pet / best part of my life / was lucky to have them – 2%
Visiting where they're buried / closure with burial process – 2%
Writing letters to my passed pet – 1%
Performing a ritual for my deceased pet (ie lighting candle daily) – 1%

Keening (Gaelic tradition) at night – 1%
Joining a NFP organization to prevent the Librela shot from harming other pets – 1%
New nephew was named after my passed pet – 1%
Started a canine rehab business in their honor – 1%
Listening to audio recordings of them purring and me talking to them – 1%

Other animals – 38%
Adopting / getting a new animal (sometimes right away, sometimes years later) – 21%
Having & loving other pets that were already in the house – 10%
Fostering a new animal – 3%
Volunteering at a local animal shelter – 2%
Shower friends' pets with love – 1%

Support from other people – 21%
Loved ones (ie supportive spouse, resilient kids, good friends) – 12%
Support group (ie Facebook pet loss groups) – 2%
Therapy – 2%
Social media accounts for pet loss support – 1%
Pet loss group therapy – 1%
Pet loss sub on Reddit – 1%
Hearing about others' pet loss grief experiences – 1%
APLB support chat – 1%

Nothing; I'm not healed yet – 14%

Time – 14%

Self care – 12%
Resources from grief experts (ie webinars, podcasts, books) – 2%
Journaling – 2%
Meditation – 2%
Crying – 2%
Wellness / self-care services – 1%
Time off work – 1%
Confronting emotions of grief – 1%
Time in nature – 1%
Recognizing that it's difficult to see signs of illness in pets – 1%

Comfort about end of life decisions – 6%
Knowing suffering is over – 2%
Knowing I made the right decision – 2%
Knowing I was there to hold them at the end – 1%
Opting for at-home euthanasia – 1%

Staying busy – 3%
New hobbies, keeping busy – 2%
Working long hours – 1%

What do you wish you'd done differently in your grieving process, if anything? (n=121)

Nothing; I don't know; I feel good about what I did to grieve – 40%

Processed things differently – 19%
Asked for help (ie talk to a therapist, join a support group) – 4%
Forgiven myself earlier; not blamed myself – 3%
Talked about it more openly – 3%
Cried more; cried in front of others – 2%

Grieved more – 2%
Not been as sad for so long - my dog wouldn't have wanted that – 1%
Did energy healing work sooner – 1%
Hadn't been so angry – 1%
Had taken time off of work – 1%

Honored my pet – 6%
Kept the ashes – 2%
Cremated instead of burying them – 1%
Had a ceremony or celebration of life – 1%
Had rituals set up to help me – 1%
Remember that we did give her a good life – 1%
Still want to get a tattoo – 1%

Regarding a new pet… – 4%
Adopted / gotten a new dog sooner – 2%
Waited longer before adopting another pet – 2%

While my pet was still here… – 3%
Spent more time with them – 1%
Considered other treatments and tried for more time – 1%
Had not trusted the vet, asked for more tests, done more research – 1%
Had not given my dog a shot suggested by the vet – 1%

Day of their death – 3%
Held them longer before we buried them – 1%
Stayed with them during the euthanasia – 1%
Had the opportunity to say goodbye (I was out of town) – 1%
Asked for a paw print – 1%

Taken better care of my own health – 2%
Not eaten so much sugar – 1%
Not drank as much alcohol – 1%

Other – 2%

Appendix 3

SAMSON'S HEALTH DATA

I created a website to share information about Samson's experience after the Librela shot. You can see his detailed health information and bloodwork results here: https://www.islibrelasafe.com.

Appendix 4

CHECKLISTS FOR DOS & DON'TS

I've included a checklist on the book's website (https://www.petlossgrief.info/resources) to provide summarized guidance for the sunset season and after your pet has passed away.

Appendix 5

RESOURCES FOR FAMILY & FRIENDS

I've included dos and don'ts on the book's website (https://www.petlossgrief.info/resources) for how to talk about pet loss death and how to support a grieving friend going through a loss.

Appendix 6

QUALITY OF LIFE SCALE (THE HHHHHMM SCALE)

Hurt
Adequate pain control, including ensuring breathing ability, is the first and foremost category on the scale. Is my pet's pain successfully managed? Is he/she breathing easily? Does he/she need pain medication?

1 = Is severely painful, is mouth beathing, or panting
3 = Is moderately painful more than 50% of the time, breathing is labored
5 = Is mildly uncomfortable less than 50% of the time, breathing is increased but not labored
7 = Is mildly or infrequently uncomfortable, breathing is increased but not labored
9 = Is completely comfortable, breathing normally

Samson's score 12 days before he passed away: 5

Hunger

Is my pet eating enough? Does hand-feeding help? Does my pet need an appetite stimulant or a feeding tube?

1 = Is not eating at all
3 = Will eat a little if coaxed
5 = Won't eat regular food, but eats well if offered baby or people food (something)
7 = Appetite is less than before, but is still interested in food
9 = Wonderful appetite, eats as well as ever

Samson's score 12 days before he passed away: 5

Hydration

Is my pet well hydrated? Does he/she need fluid therapy, either at home or at a vet?

1 = Is not drinking at all and is severely dehydrated; gums are very pale and dry
3 = Is drinking a little bit but showing signs of dehydration; gums are starting to look pale and dry
5 = Sometimes drinks normally but sometimes will not drink for long periods of time
7 = Is mostly drinking normally; gums are powdery pink and soft to the touch
9 = Is drinking normally; gums are powdery pink and soft to the touch

Samson's score 12 days before he passed away: 9

Hygiene
My pet should be kept brushed and cleaned, particularly after elimination. Bedsores must be avoided, and all wounds kept clean.

1 = My pet is severely matted (painful), has pressure sores, is badly soiled
3 = My pet is moderately matted, or coat is soiled
5 = My pet has a few small mats, but his/her skin and coat are clean
7 = My pet is not grooming as well, but I am able to keep coat and skin clean and wound-free
9 = My pet is grooming himself/herself normally; he/she has no wounds

Samson's score 12 days before he passed away: 7

Happiness
Does my pet express joy and interest? Is he/she responsive to stimulants (family, toys, etc.)?

1 = Is isolated more than 50% of the times; shows no interest in previously enjoyed activities
3 = Is spending 50% of the time isolated; Seems depressed, lonely, anxious, bored, and/or afraid
5 = Spends some time alone, but still likes to spend time with family
7 = Is still interested in old activities but cannot always perform them
9 = Has normal mobility; plays as well as he/she did before becoming ill

Samson's score 12 days before he passed away: 7

Mobility
Can my pet get up without assistance? Does he/she need human help? Is he/she having seizures or stumbling?

1 = Is no longer able to make it to the litterbox/outside on their own; soils himself/herself
3 = Activity is decreased by more than 50%, but can still make his/her way to food and litterbox/outside
5 = Ability to play, jump, run, and do normal activities is decreased by less than 50%
7 = Ability to play, jump run, and do normal activities is decreased by less than 25%
9 = Has normal mobility, plays as he/she did before becoming ill

Samson's score 12 days before he passed away: 5

More Good Days Than Bad
When there are too many bad days in a row, quality of life may be comprised, and euthanasia should be considered. Bad days may be filled with undesirable experiences such as vomiting, nausea, and diarrhea.

1 = My pet has no good days
3 = My pet has 4-6 bad days per week
5 = My pet has 2-3 bad days per week
7 = My pet has 1 bad day per week
9 = My pet only has good days and no bad days

Samson's score 12 days before he passed away: 7

A score of 5 and over is acceptable in each category. When the score drops below 5, intervention may be necessary. If further intervention is not possible and all options have been tried, then euthanasia should be considered. "One day, you will just know it's the right time because your pet will tell you with a look or gesture, a sign, or a series of bad days."

It is important to remember that the decision to euthanize a terminally ill patient is not a failure. It is a humane and loving treatment option that will prevent needless suffering.

Credit for this resource: Thrive Pet Healthcare Specialists
Originally adapted from Dr. Alice Villalobos, A.E., "Quality of life scale helps make final call," Veterinary Practice News, September 2004.

Appendix 7

MONEY SPENT ON VET, SUPPLEMENTS, MEDICINE, & DIET DURING SAMSON'S SUNSET

Date	Company/Vendor	Items	Cost ($)
April 29	Vet	Exam, Lepto Vaccine, Anal Gland Expression, Senior Blood Panel, 3 cytology, nail trim	691
May 2	Vet	Exam, Bile Acids Panel, Ultrasound, Cerenia Injection, Dex SP injection, Anti-nausea meds, appetite stimulant meds	1,408
May 2	Animal Essentials	Cordyceps mushroom tincture, mushroom defense tincture, liver defense tincture	109
May 2	Mushroom Wisdom	Maitake mushroom tincture	100
May 2	Grocery Store	Health food	112

Date	Company/Vendor	Items	Cost ($)
May 4	Best Natural Pets	Yunnan Baiyao Capsules	40
May 4	Mara Labs	Broccoli & Curcumin Capsules	110
May 4	Amazon	*The Dog Cancer Survival Guide* (book)	8
May 4	Chewy	Liver defense powder, pill pockets, healthy treats, dental treats	150
May 5	Amazon	Dog peanut butter (3) + dog ice cream	61
May 5	Chewy	Apocaps	47
May 6	Grocery Store	Rotisserie Chicken (2) + alkaline water	75
May 6	Just Food for Dogs	Specialty prepared dog food	99
May 6	Amazon	Elbow pads	14
May 7	Specialty Vet	Oncologist appointment + meds	824
May 13	Vet	Acupuncture	427
May 14	Vet	Fluids, X-rays, Appetite Stimulant Medicine	431
May 14	Pet Store	Treats	72
May 16	Vet	Acupuncture	120
May 16	Pet Store	Treats	33
May 16	Euthanasia Vet	Down payment for euthanasia & cremation	275
May 20	Euthanasia Vet	Balance for euthanasia & cremation	620
TOTAL			$5,826

Appendix 8

SAMSON'S STORY, WHICH I READ TO HIM ON MAY 17TH

Dearest Samson,

Your story started many years prior, but your story with me as your mommy began in June of 2017. You see, I hadn't yet had a dog as an adult, but I knew it was time. And I had been pet-sitting all kinds of dogs on Rover to get a sense for what type of dog I should adopt. There was this beautiful chocolate Lab named Penelope who was about five years old. I called her Lopey. I loved her. And she made me realize I wanted to adopt a senior Lab. So I found the Chicagoland Lab Rescue and told them I would like a senior Lab to foster and potentially adopt once I found the right one. They suggested I go on their website to find a dog, and there were literally dozens of beautiful dogs—how could I pick? I said, actually can you just select one of the older ones for me, so long as they are kid friendly, dog friendly, and would be ready for pickup on August 5th?

A few weeks later, I was watching Lopey again, and we were in Bickerdike park by my condo. A young husky was with his dad, and this boundless young pup really made an impression on me. I was watching him play, and I kept calling him Samson, which was strange because I knew his name was Jamo. It happened so often that day I was there with Lopey that I even thought to myself how weird it was. Fast-forward another few weeks and I was waiting in line for ice cream at Jeni's in Wicker Park. A lady in front of us was holding a little brown mutt who was very cute. My friend, a big talker, chatted her up and asked out of the blue, "Is your dog's name Samson?" I looked at my friend bewildered and asked, "Where did you get that name?" "I don't know. It just popped into my head." "So weird because I have randomly been thinking of that name!" I replied.

The day came! I had a new email from Kim at Chicagoland Lab Rescue! She said, "We have found your dog. He's a super sweet 6- or 7-year-old yellow Lab. He loves long walks and has a thyroid condition so he's on medicine. He is very friendly, and he will be ready to pick up on August 5th from his current home, as his mom was just diagnosed with cancer and can no longer care for him. His name is Samson." I about fell out of my chair!

Aunt Laura picked me up on August 5th in her Red Ford SUV, and we drove to Andersonville to get you, my very first foster dog. Your family was out of town, but the housekeeper gave you a lot of pets and kisses and thanked you for being such a good boy. We grabbed your bed and a few other items they were sending with you, and you jumped into the SUV with us. You sat right in the middle of the backseat the whole way home. I kept looking back at you and couldn't believe how lucky I was!

Within twenty-four hours of picking you up, I knew you were my dog. So loving. So sweet. Such a beautiful soul. I emailed Kim and said, "I am going to adopt him!" And from that day forward, I have been your third mommy, and you have been my first son.

We would go on lots and lots of walks. One of your favorite places was Bickerdike Park. I let you run off leash and hang out with the other doggies whenever you liked. And you were a crowd favorite, my boy. You loved to run the fence line back and forth, back and forth, until you were ready to poop. It was one of your things!

We went on our first trip to the beach with Aunt Laura and Cooper. You loved to stand belly deep in the water. Cooper taught you how to bite the water while walking around. After a handful of beach trips, I realized you didn't ever swim out further so I thought we might try swimming lessons, seeing how you are a Labrador Retriever and your tail is as big as a rudder. It was very clear from the lessons that you were a unique Labrador, one who wasn't as fond of swimming as many of your Lab friends. They said some dogs might take up to ten lessons to get the hang of it, but nah, that didn't seem like a fit for us.

You were the best host for so many dog friends who stayed with us—Charlie, Bravo, Kedzie, and even Penelope, who inspired me to foster and adopt you!

You taught me how to love unconditionally, and you have loved me unconditionally from the very beginning. I knew you had separation anxiety, and how could you not—two of your loving families had already given you up for adoption because they could no longer care for you. But I knew from our beginning—you would be with me until the end. I would be your last mommy. And speaking of love, you came to me at a time when I was looking for love. I am confident that you being in the picture led me to the man who became your daddy. We met him just three months after I adopted you.

Do you remember when he brought you a toy? And I had to tell him you don't really play with toys? Sometimes antlers. And sometimes sticks. But no toys. You've always preferred pets and adventures to anything else.

We'd go on long walks through the neighborhood with Cooper, Aksel, and Barron. You were handsome gentlemen and good friends. You are the last one of the bunch left, and they will all be waiting for you when you cross the rainbow bridge—ready to go on the next pack walk as good, good friends.

You had some fun times with the kibble vault. You were very, very food motivated, and so I had to buy a special bin for your food—one that would be hard for you to crack into. But you were determined. One time, you chewed the corner off of it, and I put a piece of purple duct tape over the hole. A few days later when Cooper was over and you two were home alone, you must have decided to get rambunctious. I don't know who instigated it, but Aunt Laura and I came home to more gnawing on the kibble vault and a piece of purple tape stuck to Cooper's butt. Oh how we laughed. And then remember the time mommy and daddy had to leave a party they were at when a review of the dogcam revealed you'd finally broken into your vault. You were eating and eating and eating. You ate so much in fact that you pooped SIX times the next day. What a silly boy!

Then there was the time that Mommy and Aunt Laura met up at a dog park on Christmas Day. It was pretty warm for December in Chicago. Cooper, Lilly, Willa, and June were all there with us. I remember that day fondly. We had lots of dog park trips to meet Aunt Laura. You always loved seeing the red SUV pull up. In fact, you always got excited when we passed a similar car parked on the street, hoping she was coming to see you.

SAMSON'S STORY

In mid-2018, we moved to a new condo a few blocks to the west. You loved that condo. You were always jumping up on your gray couch there, and sometimes you'd put your head on the big sill to look out the window at passersby a few stories down. You had a bed under the counter and between the couch—it was a favorite little cave of yours to retreat to. And sometimes you'd sleep in your bed that was in our room. But if you decided to sleep somewhere else and our bedroom door was closed, you learned how to "doink" the knob with your head and come in every morning to wake us up for your kibble and walk. I loved that sound so much. And it always put a smile on my face to greet the morning with you at my bedside.

You loved to sit outside on the double-chaise lounge at that condo. Getting the breezes and good sniffs as often as you liked. One of our favorite things you used to do there was run up the front stairs and then wait on the second-floor landing to check and make sure everyone was behind you before you finished the trek up.

And who could forget Ziggy—your best friend in the neighborhood. You loved to walk by Ziggy's house and hope that he was outside. You woo wooed for him, and the two of you just loved each other. One time we walked by and missed him, but we heard him bark—he was calling you back to say hello. You were always so excited to see your buddy.

Then there are the chickens. Someone in West Town had a gaggle of chickens who would scoot around the alleys. If you saw one, you were instantly amped up. One time, they were behind the fence where they lived and you jumped up on the fence despite your bad hips and woo wooed at them. You must have something for chickens, because there is also that time we passed the live chicken place and you were beside yourself that a chicken was flapping around in a bag on the floor.

Your story with Penelope lived on because she also stayed with us in the condo. She rehabilitated you after a scary dog bite and re-instilled your faith and love of dogs. For that, we are forever grateful to her.

It was so fitting that you got to meet Bryan and Natalie's dog, Delilah. Every Samson needs a Delilah. And even though you peed in her house (you have never done that before or since!), it was quite a joy to see you two sweet pups together.

Remember when we would go on long walks from our condo—all the way to Eckhart or Smith Park? We would take an hour or two on weekend mornings and let you go play with pups off leash. You loved to explore neighborhoods and meet dogs passing by. Some other friends of yours were Sampson, Chuey, Charlie, and Chili. And who could forget Batman and the little ceramic pig you would also whine at when we passed by? You loved to come with Aunt Michelle and me on our long walks up to North Avenue. One time it was so hot that you stopped at a storefront for shade, and we had to call Daddy to pick us up!

There were many more trips to the dog beach in the summer. And in the winter, my how you loved the snow. I remember the first time I saw you run through the snow. You were bounding like a puppy!

You still got into some things just like a puppy would. You loved to grab the toilet paper roll and run down the hallway. You unwrapped one of Daddy's Christmas gifts one time. You ate a box of Kleenex and left the mess all over the condo! Then there was the walk we

SAMSON'S STORY

went on when you grabbed not one, but TWO, dead birds off the ground. You wouldn't let go! And boy did Mommy scream so loud when you did that!!

When you were so excited to go out or when we would come home after a long day away, you would do a happy dance with your front paws. Pitter patter, pitter patter, with a big smile on your sweet face. You also liked to play bite our hands when we got the leash ready to go outside. It was your favorite! And of course—the woo woo. You didn't start doing this until around two years after you were adopted, but it was the epitome of joy. You'd throw your head back and go "WOO WOO" as loud as possible. When you were really, really happy, you'd add in a little hop and do it on repeat. You became known to some people as Woo Woo. Uncle Paul still calls you that. 😊

You came with me to my two offices a few times—you liked to sleep on my floor mat and mosey around and get pets from anyone who would give you attention.

Speaking of pets, do you remember when we went to Aunt Bailey's for Thanksgiving a few years ago? Mommy and Daddy stopped at a bar on the way home with you. You worked the entire set of patrons sitting at the bar. You got all the popcorn you could ever want that night, and you were the belle of the ball.

You loved to go with Mommy and Daddy to eat on patios or hang out in the backyard at a neighborhood cafe. You were always hoping another dog would come up and say hello to you! One night at Happy Village, you even inspired another patron to leave and come back with her dog Snoopy.

We used to watch Madeline sometimes, and the two of you were always so weirded out when Mommy would do exercises. You'd sit on my yoga mat and make it next to impossible for me to do anything, but I wouldn't have had it any other way.

In early 2019, Daddy proposed to Mommy. I came home from work on a Friday, and there you were with a sign around your neck that read "Mommy will you marry daddy?" I loved that you were such an integral part of our family's love story.

We'd go and visit Aunt Laura at work in her South Loop pet store. You ran around trying to grab all the treats you could. One time you succeeded with a very, very long Slim Jim-looking treat. I let you get it, of course. And you'd jump up on the counter when Aunt Laura was back there. Just like a kid in a candy store—you were a dog in a dog store my boy, and it was your dream come true!

You used to lie on your back with your paws up in the air. You'd sleep like that for hours. Or you'd hang your head off the couch or jam your snout somewhere that looked painful—but you loved it. Sometimes your legs would move so much during a nap that we liked to say you were "chasing bunnies." So many good naps were had!

Mommy and Daddy took engagement photos in West Town, and you were the star of the show. I love the one where you lead the way across the street while traffic was stopped, and the one where you are out ahead of us on the sidewalk pulling us to go faster and explore more. And of course, the one where you look like you are smiling with closed eyes. Such a photogenic boy!

On September 19, 2019, you were the best man in Mommy and Daddy's wedding. You wore a custom bowtie that matched Mommy's dress. You had a special white leash, and Aunt Laura walked you down the aisle. We are so grateful you were part of our big day, Samson!

And of course you were coming on our honeymoon with us. Mommy found a place named Honey-moon Farm on Airbnb. It was located in Lanesboro Minnesota, just southeast of Minneapolis. Honeymoon Farm was a magical place, and we were so lucky to be there for a whole week with you. We walked the 100-acre property many times; in fact, one time you ran off and we couldn't find you for a minute! I have a feeling Elwood's spirit was there and convinced you to cause a bit of trouble.

Mommy and Daddy put on waders and walked through the creek with you. You really liked that except for when you couldn't touch the bottom! We walked through the cute little town and had lots of meals outside with you. You became quite famous inside the art gallery as well. We went to the park where you really surprised Mommy and Daddy by jumping in a pond after some ducks! We played tennis one day, and you wanted to be part of the action on Daddy's side. We made fires at night and loved that you were there with us. We still talk about this as being one of our favorite trips ever.

Later that year, we did another big road trip to see Grandma and Grandpa in Rhode Island. We even stopped to see Aunt Tracy and Uncle Ed on the way! This was your first time in the ocean! My how you loved it on that sunny winter day! When we made it to Grandma and Grandpa's, you enjoyed hanging out in their yard and chewing on sticks. We went on long walks to where Daddy used to go to school when he was a boy. And you got a prime rib bone from Grandma. Even though Grandma is notorious for not being a dog person, we knew how much she loved you when we spied her talking to you outside when it was just the two of you. Grandpa still talks about how you did your puppy run to him on that trip—you have always had a way of making people feel so special and loved.

By the beginning of 2020, we ditched the stairs and bought you a house. It was a complete fixer-upper, so we knew there were a string of road trips in our future. The first one that year was a week-long trip to Southern Illinois. We went on hikes, searched for antiques, and we even went to a "farm zoo" where you could meet all the pigs, horses, and goats to your hearts content. You were allowed to go up and say hi to all of the animals, well, except for the guinea fowl. Which were your favorite. There is quite a trend in your history with loving birds my boy!

Later that year, the construction on our house started, and we began our seven-month stint in Airbnbs. You got to go everywhere with us during this time. After a few weeks in an Airbnb not too far from our new Chicago house, we left for Kansas City. One night there and then on to Nixa. You loved the creek and the path through the field that we walked as much as we could. Next up was Lampe in the Ozarks. A sleepy little lake town where you got to ride around in Uncle Mike's golf cart and meet the neighborhood dogs, like Murphy and that little husky pup that really got you going! Mommy has so many videos of you playing with the husky one night— you were in heaven. You always have loved huskies! And retrievers. And little white dogs. And really, all dogs...

We then headed to Arkansas and stayed on a property that had a horse who often hung out right by the backyard. You would run back and forth and woo woo at the horse—you loved having a horsey friend. From there, we went over to Oklahoma and stayed with Amy and Raegan. You got to ride in a side by side while visiting your first ranch. Mommy made you wear a silly Yoda costume for Halloween and you got to go trick-or-treating with Rory, who was dressed up as very cute two-year-old UPS driver.

On to a ranch in Texas that had a very interesting Old Western town on the property. Not to mention pygmy goats, more horses, and even llamas! One night we did a fire there, and you couldn't seem to settle down. Daddy was astonished when you flushed out an armadillo—your very first 'dillo!!! We walked in the pasture with the llamas and around the pond and had a grand time!

We drove down to Austin and stayed in a little house on a property that had road runners! Every day we drove you to a park so we could walk the path. It was so fun, minus those pesky sharp burrs that kept getting stuck in your paw. We went on a hike through some forest trails one day, and lo and behold—you spotted a deer, and we have never seen you run so fast, Samson! I still have some rocks I collected on that hike and will remember it always.

We met up with Blanca and Ben at Jesterking's outdoor brewery. It was such a cool property, and they even had about thirty goats!! You really wanted to play with the goats, but the pretty guardian dog wasn't going to let you anywhere near her herd 😊

We started our drive back north and made our way to Nashville. We got to walk to coffee shops and hang out in the backyard of the cool old bungalow we stayed in there. Even though it was COVID, we got to see Aunt Renata and meet Uncle Tim one night—an outdoor fire and lots of pets while lying in the cool grass!

From there we headed to Indy and then back to Chicago and hung around there for a few weeks—we got to stay in a house whose backyard opened up to a city park! Lots and lots of walks in the snow there. It was a beautiful place to spend time with our sweetest of boys.

Just before Christmas, we headed out for the second leg of our trip. We started with a stopover in Cleveland, where you met the pretty black Lab named Bella. Then we headed to the Catskills in NY for nearly a week in a cabin. Can you even believe we got snowed-in right after we arrived! The snow was up to your chin. We had to shovel out paths so you had somewhere to walk and go to the bathroom. Lots of cabin time and wood stove fires there.

Next, we drove to Rhode Island to see Grandma and Grandpa again for Christmas! You loved sitting on their red couch that trip. We walked a golf course with Uncle Mike and Cousin Tre.

Our next stop was Massachusetts where we met Aunt Bailey and Madeline for New Year's in a sleepy little beach town. We walked through the town and down to the beach every day, at least once. You loved the cool water and the salty ocean breeze!

It was time to go south, so we went to an Airbnb in Baltimore where we were able to see Aunt Kaitlin and Uncle Greg in their yard for a fire one afternoon. You really wanted to meet your kitty cousin Milo, but we were only allowed to say hello through the window. You've always loved kitties—they've gotten many woo woos from you!

Next up was a country setting in Swoope, Virginia. It was a huge farmhouse that had lots of land and cows! Uncle Jeff and Berkely, the Golden Retriever, met us there. We got to go on lots of hikes with Berkely and Uncle Jeff, and you loved to lie on the loveseat with Mommy by the fire in the den.

We drove to the north woods of Georgia and met Uncle Zach for a few days in Ellijay. That was a neat place! The backyard was so steep, but you liked to walk to the bottom and explore with Daddy. Then there were all the hikes through the roads near there that went up and down, up and down. It was always so fun to walk around new places!

We started our drive back to Chicago because it was almost time to move into our new house. We stopped in Cincinnati to see some of Mommy's friends and then to Michigan City for a few nights, and to Momence where Peggy, Paul, Laura, Cooper, and June met us for a visit. Then, to our very own bungalow which you would call home for the rest of your life.

Looking back, one of the most memorable parts of the trip is how many times we had to tell you that you were the "most preciousest" of our cargos. We had a very full car, and you were always keen to be right by it when we were packing up. You didn't want to be left behind, but you see, you were always the most important thing in that car. I don't know if I will ever be able to say goodbye to that car now that we have shared so many memories with you in it.

In Chicago, we built you your very own ramp so you never had to worry about stairs again. You got to sit out in the front yard and meet people passing by. You and your buddy Jackson ruled the street for a few years! You had friends come over—like Lucy and Stella. It was always so fun to open our home to other dogs. You even let Mommy and Daddy foster other dogs! There was Lucy Linna, Duke, Ellie, the Roly Polies, and of course Dolly. Dolly always lost her mind when Daddy would lift you onto the couch—she couldn't believe you were flying, Samson!

You continued to love your walks here in our Chicago neighborhood. One of our favorite things was for one of us to hold you back by the yard and then the other would stand by the road, yell "Go," and see you lope like a puppy down the gangway, so overjoyed we'd get to go on a walk together. We'd pass lots of great dogs around these parts—Russell, the greyhounds, Flow, Big Murphy, Augie (you were his first friend you know), Jackson, Padfoot, Cain and his brothers, Connie, Trevor, the girls, Murphy, Tinkerbell, Bindi, and so many more. Remember the time around Halloween a few years ago when you decided to lie down in the zombie yard? I think you were trying to figure out why all the people were crawling on top of the house! It is one of my favorite pictures to this day.

You loved the mornings when we would walk all the way to the nearby park, or sometimes we would drive there too. We would get out of the car, and you didn't even need a leash on because you are such a good boy. You'd start sniffing the ground and make your way out to the middle to see all the dogs. It was always a good day to be out there. Lots of woo wooing. You loved to see Kaleesi, Livi, Bruno, Hans, Bogey, and all of your other good friends. Getting pets from the people was also so fun.

You've always made a huge impression on people. My very favorite is "hey little baby" lady. We don't even know her name, but for the past three years, she sees you and says, "Hey little baby, Hey mister," and she loves on you so much. She kisses your head and spends minutes with you before we go our separate ways. She finally told us one day that she'd had a yellow Lab just like you and it made her so happy to see you around the neighborhood.

One summer, we drove to Pittsburgh to see Aunt Kaitlin for her fortieth birthday. We put the windows down pretty often on that trip. You loved to sit up, look out the window, and let the wind flap your pretty velvety ears. Such good smells on those trips!

Two years ago, Mommy and Daddy decided it was time to adopt a puppy for you. We wanted you to be around a young dog who could be a friend and keep you feeling young for as long as possible. You welcomed baby Murphy with an open heart. He loved you from day one, sitting right on top of you. We have dozens of memories and photos of Murphy lying right beside you. Even though he would have loved for you to play games with him, he was so grateful to have your companionship through it all. He's absolutely cherished having you as his big brother who has always been there for him.

"Beep beep beep." One of your absolute favorite things was trash day. Hearing the beeping of Mr. Bobby's trash truck as he reversed down our alley was enough to get you out of a deep sleep and beg to go outside to the yard. You'd run down your ramp as fast as possible and wait for the handful of Milk-Bones Mr. Bobby would throw you. Even though they're not the healthiest treats, we decided to let you eat as many Milk-Bones as you liked since you loved this tradition so, so much. You will always have a special place in Mr. Bobby's heart.

You showed Murph so much that you already knew and loved—the dog beach, the park, long walks, and eventually road trips. When Murphy was about seven months old, we took a family road trip to

Georgia for Mommy's fortieth birthday. Lots of Mommy and Daddy's friends came, and you got to see everyone—Aunt Bailey, Aunt Tracy, Uncle Taylor, and many more. We went on hikes and had fires at night. And once the birthday weekend was over, we took a family trip through Tennessee, stopping in Chattanooga, Knoxville, and Nashville. Lots of hikes, trips to dog parks, visits with horses and mules, and car trips to explore the area. Mommy and Daddy were hoping to find a place where we might build a second home for you and your brother.

And find it we did! In early 2023, we took you and your brother back to Tennessee to check out your new property. You got to walk back by the barn and river and take poops anywhere you wanted—and we didn't even pick it up! Mommy and Daddy loved how much you enjoyed yourself there. And your brother really liked being with you—he could have laid anywhere on that giant property, but he always chose to be right by you.

You made good friends with Mrs. Tracy, the cleaning lady. She loved coming over every Friday and seeing you. She loved how you would get up and come over to her, or how you'd give you her paw when you were laying down. She says she was drawn to you right away and has loved you so much since.

We got to go to some reunions with Murphy's siblings—I bet that was crazy for you to see so many other pups who remind you of your brother! You also got to try acupuncture, and you continued to love to go on car rides around Chicago and feel the wind on your snout and in your ears. You got to see Aunt Laura's new house and big yard with lots of good grasses.

SAMSON'S STORY

You took up the practice of going outside all the time. Your baby brother taught you how to hit the back door when you wanted to go out. Some days you would do it all day. When you got back inside, you stood by the laundry room, which I'm sure you call the treat room, and wait for something good to be shared by Mommy or Daddy. You got so many treats my boy!

Let's see, what were your favorite treats. Bobby's Milk-Bones of course. Chicken hearts. Beef livers. Duck duck goose patties. Cod skins. French fries and Wendy's breakfast potatoes. Dog ice cream. Anything from Mrs. Grace. You were always so good about taking your pills—you loved the peanut butter so much. And at night, we would give you a "brush your teeth" treat which you gobbled up and often times got two. Remember when we used to give you the kong toys with kibble in it when we'd leave? You'd have to hit it with your nose or paw to make the "kibbies" fall out a few at a time.

In October of 2023, we took a family trip down to Tennessee to check on the construction. We went to the town square nearly every day and got to walk around while brother was always eyeing the squirrels. We took lots of road trips to shops and Lowe's and dog parks. We found a great park where we could walk by the river off leash—it was so beautiful there.

Just a few months later on Christmas Eve, we packed up our car and left Chicago for our first season in the cabin. Mommy and Daddy were so excited for you and your brother to be able to live on the land we had bought for you. You had your very own ramp to the front door, but we also built the house with a walkout basement so you could be with us anywhere in the house at any time you wanted. We loved to walk the property with you. Your favorite was back by the river where the grass was so very soft on the winding path. You liked to walk a few steps into the creek with your brother too. Mommy and Daddy bought you a side-by-side so we could take family rides whenever we wanted. Mommy would sit in the back with you while Daddy would drive and brother would be running alongside us, which he loves. Remember the big snowfall we had in January and how fun that was to play in??

We took car trips to the square and the dog park and sometimes Lowe's. You got to go to therapy with Dr. Roni. She and Mrs. Angie and Mrs. Jamie just loved having you as a patient for laser therapy and hydrotherapy and shockwave therapy.

And one of the absolute best things about our days in Tennessee was when people would come visit us. Aunt Peggy, Uncle Jeff, Aunt Laura, and Uncle Steve all came to see you. And Aunt Renata and Uncle Tim came a bunch of times too. You loved to greet Mrs. Sharon. Then there was the Magic Dog Bus. You absolutely loved seeing Mrs. Amy and Mrs. Jennifer pull into the driveway in the dog bus. You'd always come out and see them. We knew you loved it so much that Mommy took you on two field trips on the dog bus. That was so fun to be able to ride along with Murphy and the other pups. You always got a yummy pup cup at the end of the field trip.

Mommy loved to sing you. At nighttime, it was a version of the Goodnight song from The Sound of Music. "Goodnight my boy my sweet angelic puppy. Sweet dreams my sweet yellow Labrador. Good night. Good night. Good night." And then I'd say "Good night my love. Mommy loves you." Our morning song has always been "Good morning. Good morning. Mommy loves you. Mommy morning. You're your mommy's baby angelllllllllll." We had versions of songs for you to "Earth Angel," "I Wanna Dance with Somebody" (I wanna dance with some puppy who loves me), "Sister Christian" (he's motorin'), "Private eyes" (are watching you), and "Lollilop" (My Samson dog Samson dog, o o my Samson dog). And I'm sure many more beyond these.

Your name has always been Samson. Of course we kept that, and you had so many good nicknames—Earth Angel. Big Yellow. Big Guy. Amarillo Grande. Simmie. Simpson. Samuel. Sam. Sammie. Samsonian. Samsonite. Bugger. Lion. Mommy's Lion. This list is so fitting that it starts with you as my earth angel and ends as my lion. You have always been and always will be both my sweet boy.

There are so many more things we could talk about in your life's story. How you loved to walk right through bushes mornings after a good rain, how the boy living on the first floor of our condo building loved you so much that he named his stuffed yellow dog Jamson, the many comments on your big beautiful paws, Daddy's love of your black mark under your left eye, how you loved busy street traffic and preferred to walk on main roads, how I cherished you coming to wake Mommy up in the cabin by asking for morning pets, and so much more. Daddy's friend, Uncle Mike, is so right—you have lived a truly elite life. A magical life. You found me in a magical way. And even here at the end, you used your magical ways to make us drive by Mommy's old condo at the exact time that your friend Charlie was walking by. It was a chance encounter that happened just as we were wondering if he was around after all these years. So you got to say hi to Charlie again, and it was even crazier that Jamo, the husky who I'd called Samson nearly seven years ago, was watching all of it from his window above.

I always knew this day would come my sweet, sweet boy Samson. I know you aren't scared and that you are planning to come back as a puppy when we are in Tennessee. We are so grateful to have known you as Samson and to have had the honor of calling you our son. You are one in a million, and we will cherish your story for the rest of the days of our lives. Until we meet again. Good night, my boy, my sweet angelic puppy....

Appendix 9

MORE PHOTOS OF SAMSON

Samson was a star in our proposal story!

Engagement photo with Samson.

At our wedding with Samson—his bowtie matched my dress!

Before we had Samson's car, he loved to ride shotgun in Daddy's jeep!

Sleeping on his favorite gray couch.

Exploring the Ozarks.

Staying warm by a fire in Ellijay, GA.

One of our more memorable walks was when Samson took an unexpected pit stop near the zombie installation a few weeks before Halloween.

Murphy still loved to lie by Samson even as he got older.

A neighborhood stroll with Daddy during sunset.

ABOUT THE AUTHOR

Gale Wilkinson is a dog mom and lover of all animals. She wrote this book on pet loss grief after Samson, her first dog as an adult, passed away on May 18, 2024. She'd always known the day would come, but she was not prepared for how difficult it was to lose him and then pick up the pieces of her life once he was gone. Samson was light and love, and Gale knew he'd want her to share his story to help the millions of pet parents who go through their own heartbreaking losses every year.

Gale's professional background is in finance, strategy, and marketing. After graduating with an undergraduate degree with honors from the University of Notre Dame, she worked at Nielsen in new product consulting and at Orbitz in strategy and data. Upon earning an MBA with honors from University of Chicago's Booth School of Business, her career path led to starting two venture capital firms—IrishAngels and VITALIZE Venture Capital—where she's had the privilege of helping many people in her network invest in 150+ early-stage startups.

Gale is also an animal communicator and active in dog rescue. She's helped nineteen dogs so far on their journeys to a better life, many of which she fostered through Chicagoland Lab Rescue (the organization from which she adopted Samson in 2017) and more recently through Gale Loves Dogs, a non-profit dog rescue she started to honor Samson's legacy. Gale currently lives in Chicago and Nashville with her husband Matt and dogs, Murphy, Lark, and Baby Noelle.